The Tsar's Doctor

The Tsar's Doctor

The Life and Times of Sir James Wylie

Mary McGrigor

BIRLINN

First published in 2010 by
Birlinn Limited
West Newington House
10 Newington Road
Edinburgh
EH9 1QS

www.birlinn.co.uk

ISBN: 978 1 84158 881 0

British Library Cataloguing-in-Publication Data
A catalogue record for this book is available from the British Library

Typeset by Iolaire Typesetting, Newtonmore
Printed and bound by Cox & Wyman Ltd, Reading

To the memory of my friend and mentor Professor Alexander Adam FRCS, Honorary Librarian of the Aberdeen Medical Chirurgical Library, who suggested that I write this book

Contents

Contents

PART TWO

List of Illustrations

Map

Introduction

How do you write a biography of a man whose autobiography has been destroyed and who, in his native country of Scotland, is now all but forgotten?

This was the question I found myself faced with when attempting to research the life of Sir James Wylie, whose own carefully kept journal was obliterated on the order of Nicholas I, the last of the three Russian tsars to whom he was both doctor and friend.

Described as 'the most famous Scotsman in Russian service . . . [whose] name is inseparably connected with the creation of the healthcare system in the Russian Army and Navy and with training of military surgeons',[1] Sir James Wylie, as he eventually became, is today revered in Russia as the saviour of soldiers, their fate having been ignored before his time.

His statue, in St Petersburg, jerks memory alive. Yet his competence as a surgeon and administrator is shadowed by the mystery in which he was involved. Under pressure, and at the risk of his life, he perjured himself to sign the death certificate of one emperor, citing apoplexy instead of strangulation as the cause. Did he then, in later years, comply with the wish of another emperor to allow him to escape from the purgatory known to have eclipsed the reasoning of his mind?

No one will ever know, unless the discovery of new evidence brings proof of what actually happened, now nearly two centuries ago, in that remote little town of Taganrog by the Sea of Azov. Without it the events of the tragic interlude, in which Wylie was so deeply involved, must remain as mysterious as so many other incidents in the life of this incredible man.

Fortunately, although Wylie's own reminiscences of his sixty-four years in Russia no longer exist, those of another doctor – an Englishman and contemporary of Wylie's named Robert Lee – have survived.

It is in fact a miracle that Lee's writings are still in existence, for he is openly, cruelly critical of both the Russian government and the tsars. Had it been found and read in Russia during his lifetime he would almost certainly have been imprisoned, if not sentenced to death. Nonetheless despite – and indeed partly because of – his abhorrence of the subjugation of the vast majority of the Russian people, his descriptions of the way they lived and of the country itself bring a vivid picture to the reader's mind. It is therefore thanks to Lee's diary that, in the absence of Wylie's own account, an idea emerges of the vast areas over which he travelled, almost invariably with the tsar, a distance he claimed to be over 150,000 miles, and of the people with whom, over more than half a century, he became involved on both a social and professional basis.

The idea of writing about Wylie was suggested to me by my friend and mentor, the distinguished surgeon, Professor Alexander Adam FRCS, Honorary Librarian of the Medical Chirurgical Society of Aberdeen, and it was thanks to Prince Alexis Troubetzkoy, a descendant of one of the 'Decembrists' who died so bravely in freedom's cause, that I discovered Wylie's account of the last tragic days of Alexander I. Despite the fact that his memoirs were destroyed, Wylie did leave a diary, written in Russian, which was published as an article in the *Russkaya Starina* magazine. Jennifer Griffiths, Senior Library Assistant of the Taylor Institute Library in Oxford, most kindly sent me a photocopy. Doctor Kenneth Dunn, of the National Library of Scotland, then sent me an essay in German on Wylie's medical practices, written on the bicentenary of his birth, by Professor Heinz Müller-Dietz. Both the Russian and German papers were translated by Dmitri Usenko, of Clearword Limited in Essex, while Caroline Roboc translated from the French.

Thus through the help of both friends and strangers I have traced the life of a reserved and inscrutable man, who today is still remembered in Russia as the champion and saviour of soldiers about whom nobody once cared. With contemporary accounts as my basis I have tried to penetrate the darkness surrounding the personality of this enigmatic Scottish doctor, who died with the secret of what really happened to Alexander I, the tsar whose death remains a mystery unsolved.

PART ONE

The Man from America

In the spring of 1854 Doctor William Channing, an American citizen by birth, arrived in the Russian capital of St Petersburg. He came with an introduction to a man famed in that city, a Scotsman named James Wylie, who had been created a baronet in his native land and who, in the capacity of personal physician, had served no fewer than three tsars in his time.

Channing was in a hurry. War between Russia and France, now allied to Britain, seemed imminent, and he might well have to leave quickly, supposing of course he could even find a ship to take him home.

For this reason he did not tarry in making his call on Sir James. With his letter of introduction in his pocket he hurriedly left his hotel, leaving his bags packed behind him in case it should prove necessary to make a speedy departure. A hired *drosky* took him through the city, past the buildings about which he had so often heard and read: the enormous Winter Palace fronting the River Neva, now surging brown with spring floods; the Mikhailovsky Palace on the opposite bank, where, as was now generally known, Tsar Paul I had been murdered over fifty years previously; the towering needle of the spire of the Alexander Nevsky Monastery, burial place of the tsars; and the great church of St Isaac's Cathedral, with its spectacular gilded dome, still in the final stages of construction,

The doctor noted the landmarks, pointed out by the bearded driver of the *drosky* with his whip. However, totally absorbed as he was with the prospect of what lay before him, he barely noticed his surroundings. *Would he be in time?* He had been told that Sir James was near his end. He willed the ancient horse to trot faster, but to no avail.

At last the *drosky* pulled up in front of a substantial house in a street called Galerney. The American tugged at the bell rope and heard it ring inside the building. Shortly after he hammered on the door, the bell having produced no response. Was he too late? Sir James Clark, the eminent London doctor who had given him a written introduction to his even more famous colleague in St Petersburg, had warned him of Wylie's illness, calling him a very sick man. Was this apparently deserted mansion already a house of death?

Then from inside came the sound of shuffling and the door was pulled back a few inches to reveal a man, who by his dress and demeanour had to be a servant, standing with his hand upon the inside knob. The American explained his business and the man ushered him into a dark and very silent hall where he was respectfully asked to wait. The servant then disappeared into a nearby room in which he carried on a mumbled conversation with another man.

'My master will see you now,' announced the servant, coming back into the hall, and the American doctor then followed him into the room from which he had overheard the conversation taking place. The light, although brighter than that in the hall, was still dim, heavy curtains being only partly drawn. Channing could only just make out the figure of a very tall man, gaunt and grey with age, lying full length on a sofa with a rug covering his legs.

'Forgive me,' said a voice in a near-whisper, 'if I do not rise. My illness precludes much movement. I am, as you see, an invalid.'

The American handed over his letter of introduction, at which the man on the sofa merely glanced, obviously finding it hard to read. Then, propping himself on his elbow, he asked his visitor to sit on the chair placed beside his couch. The two began talking, hesitantly at first, and then with greater ease. When mention was made of a mutual acquaintance, Sir James Clark, common ground was reached and the conversation flowed more freely.

The American made his visit short, sensing the huge amount of effort it took Wylie even to talk. Nonetheless on his departure, the old Scotsman begged Channing to come again. He did so, and during the course of subsequent visits the facts of an extraordinary life story were revealed.

CHAPTER ONE

The Boy Who Ran Away to Sea

Sir James openly admitted that he had been very unruly as a boy. Unlike many of the migrants who, seeking their fortune in the eighteenth century, had found their way to Russia, he had not been raised in poverty. His parents lived in comfortable circumstances, his father running a successful carrier's business in Kincardine town, then an important port at the head of the Firth of Forth. On the profits made from the business, William Wylie was able to send William and James, the two eldest of his five sons, to the local school, which stood on the north side of Tulliallan Church.

James's mind, however, as he struggled with the Latin grammar – in those days such an important part of the curriculum – was largely elsewhere. As soon as lessons were over and the black-gowned master had rung the bell, he was off, running like a hare for the harbour to see the latest ships to have sailed up the Firth of Forth.

'A daft laddie, I was. Always wanting to go to sea.'

As he spoke the American could picture him, schoolbag dumped on the cobbles, sitting swinging his legs over the harbour wall. This to him was real life; here was a man's world. Once he had the smattering of education he supposed was necessary for a career and had managed to gather together a few sovereigns, he would be off, on one of those ships lying at anchor, to find adventure far away from home.

The late 1770s were years of opportunity in Scotland. More than thirty years had passed since the Jacobite Rising of 1745 and the country was becoming slowly more prosperous. Foreign commerce, in particular, was booming. Scottish ports, particularly on the east coast, had much trade with the Low Countries, Scandinavia, and even as far abroad as Russia. Ships sailed up the Forth to Kincardine, which at that time was even more important than Alloa as a port.

Masts crowded the harbour. Sloops and brigantines, elegant vessels built for fast sailing, towered over the mundane outlines of fishing boats with their cumbersome, mostly rust-coloured lug sails.

The harbour hummed with an excitement that must have set the blood rushing through the veins of a boy such as James. The smell of the sea, drifting in from the river, was enough to inspire visions of the wide ocean beyond the Firth, crowded with pirates and gigantic monsters. Or so said the sailors, black-bearded, brown-skinned as most of them were, who came rolling along the quays to ask in their strange, garbled languages of the whereabouts of local inns. James Wylie and his friends, always ready with information, would then try to divert and prolong the conversation by asking them for stories of where they had been.

In the harbour the clamour of shouting seamen and screaming gulls mingled with the yells and curses of the drivers and the clatter of iron-shod hooves and the grinding of wheels on cobbles as drays pulled by heavy horses, many of them owned by James's father, carried cargoes unloaded from the holds of the ships. Such a scene inspired in James a sense of euphoria. He could not wait to go to sea! But his parents had other ideas. They had not paid his fees at the local school (two shillings and sixpence or thereabouts per term for each subject) for nothing. He and his elder brother William were ear-marked for professional careers. William was to become a schoolmaster, while James, it was decreed, would study medicine, then an increasingly respectable and indeed lucrative career in Scotland, as elsewhere.

Accordingly James was sent as an apprentice to the local practitioner, old Doctor Meldrum. Pedantic and short of temper, Meldrum proved a hard task-master who had little sympathy with a boy too inclined to voice his own opinions. James was set to mundane tasks, such as grinding herbs like rhubarb, then a panacea for many ills, in a mortar. He became increasingly bored. The doctor, a martinet for discipline, chastised him, whereupon James, furiously resentful at such treatment, decided to run away to sea.

Having gathered up a few essentials, he contrived to slip out of the work room at the back of the surgery where all the medicines were prepared. No one saw him go. With his pack on his back he tramped along the metalled road beside the river feeling he had foxed everyone.

6

At Cramond, further down the Forth, he managed to find the captain of a sloop lying at anchor, who agreed to take him on as an extra hand. A delighted James hurried to get on board. He had escaped!

But he had failed to reckon on his formidable mother. This resourceful and intractable lady, born Janet Meiklejohn, was every bit as wilful as her son. Guessing his intentions, she contrived to follow in his tracks and, after locating the sloop in the harbour at Cramond, she found a boatman to take her out and who agreed to lie on his oars while she went aboard. The captain must have gasped in amazement as this woman of commanding presence, towering over him in rage, seized his newly recruited deck hand by the collar and dragged him into the waiting skiff to be rowed quickly back to the shore.

The redoubtable Janet Wylie, her son still in her firm grasp, then set forth for home. Tramping side by side, James by now cowed into silence, they headed upriver for Kincardine, a distance of some twenty miles. Their feet ached, they were tired and hungry, and now, to make matters worse, heavy clouds darkened the sky in ominous sign of a storm. Soon the wind rose. Janet pulled her shawl around her head and, stumbling on in the near darkness, took a stronger grip of James's hand. Thus they struggled through ever more torrential rain, until, utterly exhausted, they knew they must find shelter or die. Suddenly, through the blackness, came a gleam of light among some trees. It proved to come from a cottage where they were able to shelter for the night

Next morning, as the sky cleared after the storm, a passer-by called in with local news. The gale had caused havoc. Trees had fallen, buildings had lost their roofs, but most tragic of all were the losses at sea. Even in the supposedly sheltered waters of Cramond harbour a sloop had gone down. Only her mast stuck forlornly out of the water marking the grave of all who had been aboard.

Shaken by his close brush with death, the hitherto rebellious pupil went on to complete his apprenticeship with the taciturn Doctor Meldrum, primarily because this was the only way by which he could gain entry to Edinburgh University.[2]

Enrolling at the prestigious university in 1786, the young Wylie was fortunate in having among his teachers some of the greatest intellects

of the day. Among them were Daniel Rutherford, an uncle of the
novelist Sir Walter Scott, who was later to become famous as the
discoverer of nitrogen gas, and Alexander Monro 'Secundus', a
member of the Academies of Paris, Berlin, Madrid and Moscow,
who was the second of three generations of world-famous professors
of anatomy. Joseph Black, who held the Chair of Chemistry, was one
of the most distinguished chemists that Scotland has ever known and
William Cullen, the Professor of the Practice of Medicine and
Surgery, continued the method of clinical teaching introduced by
Doctor John Rutherford (brother of Daniel) who, having studied
under the famous Boerhaave at Leyden, had introduced this system
to Edinburgh University shortly after the Jacobite Rising of 1745.

Outstanding among other greatly eminent men at Edinburgh were
James Hamilton, the first Professor of Midwifery in Scotland, and
John Thomson, lecturer on Pathology, another who ranked first in
his field. Best known of all, perhaps, was Professor James Gregory,
inventor of Gregory's mixture (a laxative compounded mainly of
rhubarb) and already a household name.

Wylie matriculated in anatomy and surgery in 1786, in medical
theory and practice in 1787, and in anatomy and surgery in 1788. He
gained his practical knowledge in the Royal Infirmary in Edinburgh,
one of the most advanced hospitals of the day. The matriculation
records in Edinburgh University Library attest to Wylie's achievements over the space of three years, the usual time taken to qualify as
a practitioner at that time.

The surgical skills he gained in Edinburgh were to stand him in
good stead, and the fact that he left the university without graduating
was not unusual at the time. Adventure was all that mattered to him.
Moreover money could be made abroad. It was certainly hard to find
at home. If legend can be believed Wylie, at one time, together with
some of his equally penniless friends, was funding his exploits in the
taverns of Edinburgh by selling stolen sheep. Somehow this enterprise
was brought to the attention of the authorities, and Wylie soon
discovered that officers of the law were on his trail. Some years before
a man named Robert Livingston had been 'banished from the Shire
of Clackmannan' for the same offence and had been warned that if he
were caught again he would be subject to the death penalty.[3] Thus

with the threat of the gallows looming, Wylie, his pockets stuffed with money from the sale of the stolen animals, persuaded a farmer, who may have been one of his gang, to drive him to the docks of Leith, then the main embarkation point for Europe, hidden in his cart beneath a load of hay.

Wylie sailed for Russia by way of Gothenburg in Sweden. He then travelled on to Riga, a shipping centre in western Russia, now the largest city in the Baltic States. There he found that because he had failed to graduate in Edinburgh, he had to take an examination at the city's medical college in order to be eligible to practise as a surgeon. Having passed, he set off for St Petersburg, where, at the Medical Collegium, then the highest medical institution in Russia, he passed yet another examination, which allowed foreigners to practise there. Then, on 9 December 1790, he was assigned to the Yelets [Eletsky] Infantry Regiment as a surgeon.[4]

CHAPTER TWO

Performer of Miracles

Wylie came to Russia at a time when the country was ruled by one of the most extraordinary and dynamic women who have ever lived: Catherine the Great.

Born in the Baltic city of Stettin, Pomerania, in 1729, the daughter of Prince Christian Augustus of Anhalt-Zerbst, and his wife Joanna, Princess of Holstein-Gottorp, Sophie Augusta Frederica, as she was christened, was remarkably ugly as a child. By the age of thirteen, however, she was beginning to show signs of the beauty and sensuality which would hold so many men enthralled. Her portrait, painted by the French artist Antoine Pesne, was sent to the Empress Elizabeth, Peter the Great's daughter, and Tsarina of Russia since the death from smallpox of her elder sister's son. Unmarried herself, she was impressed by the likeness of the young Sophie, whom she thought a suitable bride for the unattractive and sickly Prince Peter Ulrich of Holstein, her nephew and heir. The marriage took place in 1745 when Peter was seventeen and Catherine, as Sophie's name was changed to, was sixteen.

Catherine was not in love with her husband but she wanted to be a queen. She soon began to take lovers, and afraid that Peter wanted to get rid of her, she agreed to participate in a plot, orchestrated by three brothers named Orlov, to have him put under house arrest. On the morning of 28 June 1762, she set off by coach from Peterhof to St Petersburg. Reaching the Winter Palace, she came out on the balcony with her young son Paul beside her, while crowds cheered ecstatically below.

Shortly afterwards she issued a manifesto to justify her reasons for subjecting her husband's power.

Firstly she claimed that Orthodoxy was being threatened by foreign creeds; secondly, that Peter had betrayed his country by making peace with Frederick the Great of Prussia, and thirdly that the country's government had been mismanaged to the point where it was no longer effective.

That evening, wearing the uniform of the Preobrazhenski Guards, and with her long flowing chestnut hair held in place by a sable-lined hat crowned with oak leaves, she mounted her white stallion, Brilliant, to ride back to Peterhof at the head of a troop of soldiers. On reaching the palace, she ordered that her husband Peter be arrested and placed under guard at Ropsha, a nearby estate. Six days later he was killed by Alexei Orlov.

Catherine, denying all involvement in his death, declared he had died of colic. It is possible that he was poisoned, but the fact that she had his head and throat covered as he lay in state prior to his burial, suggests that he might have been strangled.

Once in power the young empress, then a woman of thirty-four, proved herself an adept, though absolute, ruler. Catherine herself founded both schools and hospitals in the major cities of her realm. In doing so she was following the lead of her late husband's grandfather, who, aware of the ignorance of the Russian physicians of his day, had first brought Scottish doctors to Russia, both to educate his own practitioners and to manage the hospitals that he built.

A century had passed since Peter the Great, tsar of Russia 1682–1725, had made his epic journey to the west, returning convinced that the country's future lay in conforming economically and culturally to the models of Western Europe. The first Russian ruler to leave his own country for more than 600 years, he had gone with the main purpose of learning how to build and crew ships with the object of establishing a navy in the Black Sea. Working himself as a shipwright in Amsterdam, he had helped to build a frigate which remained in service in the Dutch East India Company for many years. Crossing the North Sea to England, he had then learned more about ship-building at Deptford and increased his knowledge of arming warships at the Royal Arsenal at Woolwich. Most notably he had induced several hundred skilled craftsmen to return with him to Russia, including Professor Ferghasen of Aberdeen University, founder of the school of navigation in Moscow.

In awareness of the medical ignorance of the Russian physicians of his day, he had also imported doctors, both to train his own practitioners and to manage the hospitals he had built, including one founded in Moscow in 1702, with a medical school attached.

As well as building hospitals and encouraging foreign doctors to work in Russia, Catherine also founded the Medical Collegium in St Petersburg, the constitution of which also encompassed the Medical Chirurgical Academy, a combined civil body which controlled the whole medical profession. The joint functions of the two institutions included lecturing, examining and licensing, control of drugs, quarantine, vaccination, stipends and appointments. At the end of the 1790s the only Russian university was in Moscow. Four more would be established within the next decade, but only by passing a separate examination (as well as signing an affidavit not to poison the tsar) could students gain a licence to practise. Later James Wylie was to be president of the Academy for a period of thirty years.

At that time the shortage of surgeons in Russia became even more acute, with the creation of numerous medical positions in the army and civil service. The situation was, indeed, so desperate that foreign emissaries of the royal court were instructed to look around for suitable doctors and entice them, with offers of financial reward, to come to Russia. Subsequently, thanks to the poverty that was rife in Scotland at the time, and to the undeniable lure of adventure, many Edinburgh University students seized on the chance to prosper overseas.

Catherine imported so many doctors, principally from Britain, that a British doctor, returning from Russia near the end of the eighteenth century, reported that 'Persons calling themselves English physicians are found in every town in Russia. Sometimes they have served in apothecary's shops in Edinburgh and London, but are generally Scots apothecaries, who are men of professional skill and acknowledged superiority.'[5] Foremost among them in the early eighteenth century was Doctor Robert Keith Erskine of Alloa, who as Peter the Great's personal physician had gone with him on his visit to the West. The sixth son of the Earl of Mar, who had led the Jacobite army in the Rising of 1725, Erskine was himself an ardent Jacobite who had found sanctuary in Russia.[6]

On his arrival in Russia, James Wylie therefore found many

compatriots who shared his profession. Among them was Doctor John Rogerson from Dumfries, attendant to the royal family; Doctor Robert Simpson, who, having joined the Scottish Admiral Greig's fleet in 1774, was now chief surgeon to the naval hospital at Kronstadt; a Doctor Leighton, chief of the Naval Medical Services Department; and Doctor Alexander Crichton, head of the Civil Department of Medicine.[7]

For ambitious and penniless young men, Russia was indeed a good place to find both advancement and fortune. Doctor Rogerson did so well for himself that he was able to retire back to Scotland to buy the estate of Wamphray and build the house of Dumcrieff in his native Dumfries-shire. Famously, Rogerson frequently received the gift of a snuff box from one of his grateful patients, which he then sold to a jeweller. The jeweller then resold it to the next noble patient, who felt himself indebted to his physician, and so the practice continued until it became so normal a transaction that the snuff box was handed over without a word being spoken or a bank note given in exchange![8]

As Wylie arrived in Russia, the war with Turkey, which had lasted for four years, was coming to an end. An attempt to drive the Turks from Europe had ended, after great loss of life, with a victory for Catherine's General Potemkin as the sultan was forced to ask for peace. By the Treaty of Jassy, signed on January 1792 (Gregorian Calendar), Russia obtained all the territory between the rivers Bug and Dniester, the Crimea and Ochakov. However, although the whole north coast of the Black Sea now belonged to Russia, the sea itself remained closed to it because the Turks still controlled the southern straits. The Empress Catherine had failed in her ambition to take Constantinople, where she had planned to install the second eldest of her grandsons – in expectation of her triumph confidently christened Constantine – as king.

Three months later, in March 1792, the King of Poland, who had already agreed to a treaty of mutual protection with Prussia, approved a new constitution. The Empress Catherine at once interpreted this as a manifestation of the same revolutionary spirit evinced by the Jacobins in Paris. On the strength of this, putting action to her words, she sent 64,000 Russian soldiers into Poland and another 32,000 into Lithuania. The Poles, in desperation, appealed for help from Prussia, but King Frederick William, despite the former agreement, now declared that he was not committed to defending a constitution drawn up in Poland without his knowledge.

Further to this, in January 1793, the King of Prussia signed a pledge with Russia providing for a second partition. The Polish Diet, under armed threat, was forced to ratify a new treaty by the terms of which Russia took the northern regions of Poland, including Vilna, Minsk and Kiev, a region of 455,000 square kilometres in all. Prussia acquired Poznan, Danzig and part of Silesia, while Austria acquired some territory as well. The Empress Catherine, then triumphant, convinced she had subdued the radical element in Eastern Europe, concluded a treaty with Poland, which totally destroyed its independence by ensuring that all its governance would be managed henceforth from St Petersburg.[9]

Although while at home in Scotland he had heard many travellers' tales about Russia, nothing could have prepared James Wylie for life in the extraordinary country that was to be his home for the rest of his days. He discovered a land of unparalleled contrasts: on one hand poverty on a hitherto unimagined scale; on the other wealth and opulence, so flamboyant that it had to be seen to be believed.

Appearance was all that mattered to the aristocratic families – or at least so it appeared. Status was judged by the number of servants in a household, in some of the greater palaces literally hundreds were employed. Nearly all were serfs, who although fed and housed, did not receive a proper wage. Competition raged as to who had the grandest carriages, the best bred horses, and as far as the women were concerned, the most opulent dresses and jewels. To Wylie, brought up in Protestant Scotland, where thrift was highly esteemed, it must have seemed that he had entered a new world, dictated by values that had previously been completely alien to him.

The treatment of the soldiers themselves was but one example of the upper echelons of society's total contempt for the common man. While there was no regular conscription, the tsar could command his nobles at will to provide serfs to fill the ranks of his army. These men, once in uniform, were treated little better than the horses for which many of them had to care, and they could be flogged to death without thought.

When Wylie arrived in Russia, the Empress Catherine had been reigning for twenty-eight years. The slim young woman with her glorious chestnut hair who, astride her white thoroughbred, had led her deposed husband's soldiers to Peterhof, was now gone. At sixty-one, and approaching old age, she had become squat and fat. Nonetheless she still held herself erect and little if anything escaped the imperious gaze of those wide-apart, brilliant black eyes.

As tsarina, Catherine held absolute power over the 37 million inhabitants of the vast country of 8.75 million square miles over which she ruled. Of that number, only the aristocrats, who totalled a mere 2 per cent, lived in any kind of comfort. The peasants, who could be given away or sold at their owner's whim, occupied the smoke-filled wooden or earthen huts of the villages, where they slept on a shelf above the stove in order to survive the winter months.

There was much famine and much feasting. The peasants lived largely on cabbage soup and potatoes, but in years of bad harvests even these staple foods failed. Tolstoy has left a heart-breaking picture of a family dying of food poisoning from eating the rotten carcass of a sheep. Conversely, the nobles, who were largely great land owners, could lavishly entertain. In April 1792, the empress's long enduring favourite and statesman, Prince Grigory Potemkin – her secret husband, or so it was believed – staged an enormous banquet in his palace of Taurida. Threatened by the ascendance of a rival for her favours, Potemkin pulled out all the stops to impress Catherine. Hundreds of actors, dancers and musicians were brought in to entertain. The empress, on arrival, walked between two rows of footmen in cream and silver livery, holding candelabras to light her way through the 3,000 guests who bowed at her approach. Potemkin himself, a one-eyed giant, looked magnificent in a scarlet coat embroidered with gold, over which was hung a long cloak of black velvet held in place with diamond clasps while his hat, too heavy with precious stones to wear, was carried behind him by a page.[10]

Three months later, in July, Potemkin left St Petersburg to prepare for a war against Poland, but on reaching Jassy he caught malaria. Desperate to leave the disease-ridden city, while travelling over the steppes of Bessarabia he asked to be carried from his carriage and died by the side of the road.

On 23 January 1793, Russia and Prussia signed the Second Partition of Poland, in which that country was reduced to only 200,000 square kilometres, containing a population of approximately four million people. The economy was ruined and support for a rising rapidly increased.

The dissidents rallied under Thaddeus Kosciuszko. The son of a small Polish landowner, Kosciuszko had been educated in Paris, where he had become imbued with revolutionary ideals before going on to America where, in the Confederate army, he had risen to the rank of Brigadier.

On 24 March 1794, in the market square of Cracow [Krakow], Kosciuszko swore an oath to liberate Poland, and the revolution against Russia began. Two months later, Kosciuszko, having been made commander-in-chief of the Polish–Lithuanian army, issued the famous Proclamation of Polaniec, famously promising freedom to the serfs who joined his rebellion. Despite initial successes, Kosciuszko was wounded in the battle of Maciejowice in 1794. Taken prisoner by the Russians, he was held in St Petersburg. His supporters fought on gallantly until they were overwhelmed by Russian might in the Polish capital of Warsaw.

Wylie is known to have been serving with his regiment at the siege of Warsaw in 1794. Commanded by General Suvorov, most brilliant of Catherine's generals, the Russian army reached the outskirts of the city on 3 November. In darkness, at three o'clock the following morning they attacked. After four hours of desperate fighting in Praga, part of the eastern section of the city, the defenders were utterly defeated. Next day, after vicious looting by the Russians during which it has been estimated that 20,000 civilians were killed, the city surrendered. Suvorov, triumphant, sent a three-word message to the Empress: *Hurrah – Praga – Suvoro*, to which she replied: *Congratulations – Field Marshal – Catherine*.

It was during this campaign that Wylie was horrified to find that it was only wounded officers who received medical attention. In most cases ordinary soldiers were simply left lying where they fell. But being a lowly army surgeon, he was incapable of doing anything to rectify what to him was an appalling situation. Nonetheless the young

Scottish doctor, insignificant at that point as he knew himself to be, determined to target men of high rank as the means of gaining his end. Ambitious to the point where he believed that time and circumstance would work a transformation on his much-neglected profession, he swore that the day would come when he would be able to ensure that the scandalous cruelty and neglect of the common soldier in the field would be a thing of the past. Meanwhile he waited, with the tenacity of a true Scotsman, for the opportunity to increase his own influence to a degree that would give him the power of manipulating higher authority to achieve his goal.

Following the victory in Warsaw, in the following year, Russia, Austria and Prussia annexed the remains of Poland among themselves. Prussia obtained the northern part of the country, including Warsaw. Austria got West Galicia, which incorporated Cracow, and Russia took the vast area from the Baltic to Volhynia. Poland, despite putting up a heroic struggle, had disappeared.

James Wylie is known to have been at Cracow with the Russian army when this so-called Third Partition of Poland was agreed. As a soldier he was an obsessive gambler, at times losing all his possessions even down to the field mattress on which he slept. But, by now fluent in Russian, his skill as a surgeon was gaining attention. Robert Lyall, one of the many fellow Scots doctors who were practising medicine in Russia, drew attention to his fellow countryman by praising him as 'an expert and successful lithotomist',[11] as the result of which he was asked to operate on several distinguished patients. Foremost among these was the Danish ambassador, Baron Otto von Bloom, in agony with a stone in his bladder which Doctor Rogerson and his colleague, a German surgeon, were in despair about using a catheter to remove. On the verge of defeat, Rogerson suddenly remembered his compatriot Wylie, who managed to improvise a trocar from the catheter and was able to perform the lithotomy which saved the ambassador's life.

Following the success of this, in February 1794 Wylie managed to draw the attention of the authorities to himself by submitting a report about his achievements to the Collegium. He wrote that he had successfully managed to treat fever with his own medicine, a 'solutio mineralis', and to remove a stone as large as a chicken's egg from a soldier's body by lithotomy, a process that was then little known in Russia. The submission was accompanied by a commendation from General Staff Doctor K.F. Scheinvogel and by a request from his regiment's commanding officer to promote Wylie to Staff Surgeon. The Collegium, while fully granting the request, yet showed little interest in the enterprising young chirurgeon.[12]

Wylie was greatly mortified by the lack of recognition which he genuinely believed he deserved. However, news then came that he had been awarded the degree of MD by the University of Aberdeen, on 23 December 1794, on the strength of which he resigned from the Russian army on 1 November 1795.

He then became medical attendant to the family of Prince B.V. Golitsyn, the Grand Duke Alexander's (Catherine's eldest grandson's) greatest friend and confidant, as well as tutor to the son of a Colonel Fenshawe, one of the many mercenaries employed in the Russian army. In addition Wylie set up a private practice, first in Moscow, and then in St Petersburg.[13]

CHAPTER THREE

The Reign of Fear

On 17 November 1796, the Empress Catherine collapsed from a stroke. Three days passed while those in the Winter Palace seemed to live in a time capsule of stunned immobility before she died.

Then, as though fired by an invisible hand, there was sudden hectic activity as the question of her successor was debated in muttered voices. Having long quarrelled with her eldest son, the Grand Duke Paul, the tsarina had wished her grandson, Alexander, to succeed her but had failed to alter her will accordingly. Therefore Alexander's father, the mentally unstable Paul, became tsar of all the Russias.

Immediately life within the Winter Palace changed. The huge house echoed to the tramping of boots and jangling of spurs as soldiers from Gatchina, Tsar Paul's estate, some twenty-five miles from St Petersburg, which, given to him by his mother he had run like an army barracks, came marching in to the building so recently hushed in sorrow following the empress's death.

Once installed in the Winter Palace, the tsar stuck to his daily routine of watching platoons of his soldiers parade. Frederic Masson, a former tutor to Alexander, described how, even in the coldest weather, the tsar, 'in a plain deep green uniform, great boots and a large hat' watched his soldiers being drilled.

> Surrounded by his sons and aides-de-camp he would stamp his heels on the stones to keep himself warm, his nose in the air, one hand behind his back, the other raising and falling a baton as he beat time, crying out 'Raz, dva-raz, dva' [one, two-one, two].[14]

Outside the palace was lined with armed sentries to the amazement of the populace, among whom rumours soon became rampant that an enemy was about to invade. Those in the Gatchina uniform included the Grand Duke Alexander who was now, on his father's orders, reduced to the rank of sergeant. Elizabeth, his young wife, wept when she saw him so strangely dressed, but he had little time to comfort her as his father fired out orders commanding him to oversee the installation of the sentry boxes along the palace walls.

One of Tsar Paul's first actions, on succeeding to the Russian throne, was to summon Colonel Alexei Arakcheev from Gatchina. This man, the son of a small provincial landowner, had proved himself so conscientious in the school of artillery that Paul had appointed him to teach the rudiments of military tactics to Alexander and Constantine, his eldest sons. Arakcheev, with his almost fanatical devotion to discipline, was later to prove a nemesis in Alexander's life. Nonetheless, at this time, when all he had known at his grandmother's court had vanished as if at the stroke of a sword, Alexander welcomed Arakcheev with tears.

So great was the new tsar's hatred of his mother that he left her beloved summer palace of Tsarskoe Selo to lie empty in a state of neglect. The palace, designed by Francesco Bartolomeo Rastrelli in the 1750s, was one of the finest buildings of that age. Soon the empty rooms were filled with dust. Weeds rampaged over the beautiful English garden, embellished with the statuary Catherine had collected, where she had loved to sit, and the Catherine Park, named after her, grew wild as it was left abandoned to uncut shrubs and trees.

In increasing defiance of his mother's rule, Paul had the embalmed body of his father, the ill-fated Peter III, disinterred from the monastery of Alexander Nevsky and transferred into an ornately decorated sarcophagus which was laid in state beside that of his mother, her complicity in his father's death being one of the main reasons she was so detested by their son.[15]

The extent to which the new tsar's mental health had deteriorated became rapidly more evident. Shortly after his succession, he forbade all imports of foreign books. Booksellers in both Moscow and St Petersburg were placed under police control, while in the cities themselves, people were arrested and searched without warrant as Paul declared police authority to be above the law.

Within the Winter Palace Paul's courtiers and his family lived in a state of constant fear. The slightest thing annoyed him – the depth of a curtsey, the cut of a collar, even the angle of a hat.

He took particular pleasure in tormenting his sons' young wives, especially Elizabeth, whose letters to her mother in Baden had to be smuggled out. He picked on her specifically when her sister became engaged to Gustav IV, the King of Sweden, who had jilted Paul's own daughter, Alexandra, an unforgivable slight in his mind.

By the spring of 1800, Doctor Rogerson, his own physician, was thoroughly alarmed. 'The cloud is darkening,' he wrote. 'The incoherence of his movements increases and becomes more manifest from day to day.'

All those within the Winter Palace, from his own family down to the lowest serf, lived in terror of the tsar. Even Count Kutaisof, the erstwhile barber, now transformed as the royal favourite, was terrified by his erratic moods. Soon afterwards, Doctor Rogerson, the kindly Scottish doctor who had known Alexander from birth, found the Grand Duke and his wife Elizabeth crying in each other's arms. So great was their terror of his father that they could only confide to each other in whispers lying in bed at night.[16]

Unpredictable and terrifying as was Paul to his daughters-in-law, the behaviour of his wife, Maria Feodorovna, was almost as bad. A bully, she rejoiced in dominating the unfortunate young women who were married to her eldest sons. Made to scurry back and forth bearing messages and carrying out trivial orders, they were treated as inferior ladies-in-waiting and subjected to tiresome and often humiliating tasks. Possessive over Alexander, she particularly resented his obvious fondness for his wife, who was young and beautiful while Maria herself, after bearing nine children, had grown fat and was losing her looks.

Seizing every chance to degrade Elizabeth, Maria chose the day of Tsar Paul's coronation in Moscow, in May 1797, to deliver one of her most hurtful jibes. Elizabeth, dressed by her ladies, had to present herself to her mother-in-law, to have her appearance approved. On impulse, she had pinned some lovely pink rosebuds to the diamond buckle of her sash. The Empress merely looked her up and down before, without a word, she pulled the roses from her buckle and threw them on the ground. '*Cela ne convient pas*' ('this is not suitable') was her only bitter remark. Elizabeth blushed crimson, trying not to give the spiteful woman the pleasure of seeing her cry, while Alexander, who happened to be in the room, stood by helpless, too afraid of the consequences to interfere, although secretly nearly choking in his rage.

Highly excitable and unbalanced as he was, the tsar became frantic when told that Count Kutaisof, now ennobled as his closest friend and confidante, was gasping to death from a deep throat abscess. Doctor Rogerson was unable to save him, but James Wylie, hearing the case discussed among other doctors, said to one of them that he believed he might be able to help. When a member of his desperately anxious family heard of this, in defiance of protocol, and to the fury of the doctors attending him, Wylie was summoned to Kutaisof's bedside.

Instantly assessing the situation, and to the amazement of those standing by, he at once performed the first laryngotomy operation ever seen in Russia. As the count began to breathe again and was obviously out of danger, the tsar, ecstatic in his gratitude, summoned Wylie to the Winter Palace the next day.

Such was the public sensation that, shortly afterwards, on the recommendation of Doctor Rogerson, Wylie was appointed court operator on 25 February 1798.[17]

The young Scotsman, forewarned of the emperor's unpredictable moods, by now a major source of gossip in St Petersburg, attended the summons with excitement tinged with apprehension. Entering the huge, rambling building, he was conducted by an equerry through a maze of passages to the sovereign's apartments. The first thing he heard, on reaching the door, was the clamorous barking of dogs. The tsar had a whole pack of various breeds which he treated like soldiers, the passion of his life, being known to beat some of them savagely whenever he felt a need to vent his wrath.

On coming into the bedroom, as the dogs sniffed round his feet, Wylie's eye was caught by rows of tin soldiers, painted in uniforms of regimental colours. These he knew from hearsay to be the imaginary army with which the tsar still played, as he had done since childhood, lining them up for mock battles on the counterpane of his great imperial bed.

As Wylie, wearing the dark green uniform of the Eletsky Regiment, was ushered into his presence, the tsar, in that of the Imperial Guard, emblazoned with decorations and gold epaulettes, extended a hand for him to kiss. Speaking in French, the language of the court, this extraordinary man with the snub-nosed features, who was none-theless one of the most powerful in the world, thanked him, with obvious sincerity, for saving the life of his friend. Wylie, his head bowed in acknowledgement, was then about to withdraw when, to his astonishment, he heard the tsar, his voice staccato with excitement, appoint him to his personal staff.

Instantly, as the tsar spoke, Wylie knew his life was about to change. He would now have a suite of rooms in the Winter Palace. He would no longer be a near nonentity, a junior member of a profession low in the social scale. Measuring his new appointment with Scottish shrewdness, he realized that if he played his cards carefully, he might rise to hitherto unimagined heights.

True to his steadfast roots, however, Wylie refused to have his head turned by this sudden change of events. A shy man by nature, and unmoved, at least outwardly, by his sudden rise in significance, he later belittled his achievements by claiming that he owed his rise in the hierarchy of the royal household to the cutting of Count Kutaisof's throat.

CHAPTER FOUR

Doctor to the Tsar

James Wylie had become surgeon to the Russian court at a time when the mental instability of the Grand Duke Paul, eldest son of the Empress Catherine, was already causing great concern.

Count Feodor Rostopchin, a courtier to whom Tsar Paul, in his deluded state, was constantly turning for advice, writing to Count Simon Vorontzov, the Russian Ambassador in London, had told him that:

> Next to dishonour, nothing could be more odious to me than Paul's goodwill. The Grand Duke's head is filled with phantoms, and he is surrounded by such people that the most honest man among them would deserve to be hanged without trial . . . One cannot see anything the Grand Duke does without being moved to pity and horror. One would think he was trying to invent ways to make himself hated and defeated . . . he seizes on anything and punishes indiscriminately. The least delay, the least contradiction, makes him beside himself and he flies into a rage.[18]

Wylie, in his new position, was soon to prove himself as much a psychiatrist as a doctor. The tsar, who was highly neurotic, swore he heard buzzing in his ears. Finding it useless to assure him otherwise, Wylie hit upon the ingenious idea of finding a bee (presumably a dead one) and inserting and extracting it, as though by sleight of hand, from one of the emperor's ears. On seeing the insect, Paul was delighted. The buzzing had totally ceased. His genius of a physician had effected yet another miracle with his skill!

Wylie is known to have been in attendance when the tsar travelled to Moscow and then eastwards across Russia to Kasan, to see for himself the city which had been rebuilt by Catherine the Great after being destroyed in a revolt by the Cossack ataman Yemelyan

Pugachev. It seems safe to imagine that it was during these journeys, when in constant close contact with Paul, that Wylie came to realize the extent of the tsar's mental instability. It was also the time when he achieved increasing dominance over this sometimes violent and at all times sadly demented man.

Following his appointment as doctor to the tsar, the Medical College had confirmed Wylie's qualifications as a doctor and surgeon in Russia, making him an honorary member.[19] On 23 June 1799, he became Surgeon in Ordinary, and the extent of his hold over Paul is revealed by the fact that, in 1799, when the Military Medical Academy of St Petersburg was launched to train doctors for the army and navy, he became its first president. His work in the improvement of the Russian hospital system is described in the *British and Foreign Medical Review* Volume 1 (1836–47) and in *The Lancet* of 7 August 1897. Further to this, by 1800, he was taking a leading part in founding the Medical Chirurgical Academy in St Petersburg. Then on 16 March 1800 the Medical Collegium, despite their previous dismissal of his submission, confirmed him as a doctor of medicine on the basis of his doctoral diploma earned from Aberdeen University and in the same year elected him their honorary member.

Seen in hindsight it is hardly surprising that the sudden rise to eminence of the handsome, if rather forbidding, Scottish doctor sent tongues wagging in St Petersburg. Some were openly sarcastic. Throughout his career in Russia Wylie was to be plagued by the jealousy of some of his confederates, resentful that a foreigner should supplant them in the favour of the tsar.

Despite an embargo on shipping – the tsar, who was anxious to collude with the French, had barred British ships from the Baltic – word of Wylie's rising predominance as physician to the royal family somehow filtered through to Scotland.

The news spread quickly over the teacups. The redoubtable Janet Wylie was not slow to spread word of the prowess of her once disgraced but now successful son. The story spread from mouth to mouth downstream from Kincardine until, in the fishing port of St Ninian's, it reached a Mrs Willox, a lady indefatigable as was Janet herself. Hearing of James Wylie's transformation – living in a palace no less – she grasped at the possible chance to save her own son.

John Willox, a sailor on a vessel named the *Ann Spittal*, had sailed from the Firth of Forth for Russia. However, on the tsar's exclusion of British ships from the Baltic, the ship had been seized and its crew imprisoned. Picturing John ill and starving in a flea-infested Russian jail, his mother, too poor to afford either a horse or a cab, but determined to save her precious son, walked from Stirling to Paisley where she bought the finest silk thread with which, in the Troy pattern, very fashionable at the time, she knitted a pair of socks.

The hose completed, Mrs Willox, illiterate herself, persuaded the local schoolmaster to pen a letter to the Tsar of Russia pleading for her son's release. Knowing that ships from Kincardine sailed for the Baltic she then found a sea captain who agreed to take the socks, together with the letter, to St Petersburg, which, somehow avoiding the boycott, he managed to achieve. There, as instructed, he gave the package to Wylie, who in turn handed them on to the tsar. The mentally unstable Paul, pleased as a child with his gift, then promptly ordered the release of John Willox, who quickly returned home.

Wylie, although often described as mean – largely because, once installed in the Royal Palace, he never bought himself a meal – was in this instance generous to a fault. Knowing young Willox to be penniless, he gave him a present of money to take home. Arriving at the little cottage in St Ninian's his mother, while overjoyed at his return, nonetheless as a canny Scots lady determined to use the financial windfall to commemorate the great event. Thus with the money, she bought a grandfather clock, the face of which bore the inscription: 'wha'd hae thocht it, stockings bocht it'.

The neighbours gathering to see this extravagant purchase now knew, as Mrs Willox poured out the tale of its inception, that James Wylie from Kincardine, wild lad as he had been, was now a man of importance in constant attendance on no less a person than the Tsar of Russia himself.

CHAPTER FIVE

The Palace of Intrigue

Wylie now found himself living in the vast building of the Winter Palace. Designed by the architect Francesco Bartolomeo Rastrelli between 1754 and 1762, it contained over 1,000 rooms. As elsewhere in similar, if smaller, residences in Europe, and indeed throughout the rest of the early-nineteenth-century world, intrigue was the main occupation of all those within the palace walls. In addition to the uniformed soldiers whom the tsar felt essential to his safety, the building teemed with servants, men wearing livery and powdered wigs and housemaids in dresses and caps. Wylie had his every need attended to by the valet who replaced his soldier servant and by the minions who scurried back and forth with hot water and coals for his fire. Known to have had almost every meal in the palace, he probably dined with the equerries, being senior to even the top servants in the strict hierarchy that was observed.

The apartments of the royal family itself included that of the tsarina, Maria Feodorovna, Grand Duchess of Württemberg, who, as the mother of eight children, had secured the inheritance of the family. Her eldest son, the charming and handsome Alexander, heir to the imperial throne, had been married in 1793 at the age of just fifteen. His bride, some ten months younger, who had been chosen by his grandmother, the formidable Catherine the Great, was the beautiful but fragile Louise, daughter of the Crown Prince of Baden, who, again on the orders of the matriarch, had changed her name to Elizabeth Alexeievna on her marriage.

Also living within the palace were Alexander's siblings: Constantine, eldest of his three brothers, who at eighteen had recently married Anna Feodorovna of Saxe-Coburg, and Nicholas, the next in age, who was still a baby, born almost as his grandmother died.

Alexander and Constantine, largely brought up by their grandmother, who had snatched them as infants from their mother's arms, had shared little of their childhood with the younger members of their family. Of the four sisters, Alexandra, Helen, Marie, Catherine and Anna, it was Catherine who, although eleven years younger than Alexander, was to prove his confidante in later years. The last of Maria Feodorovna's children, a boy named Michael, was to be born, with Rogerson and Wylie in attendance, in 1798.

Fashions were changing in Russia, influenced by countries in western Europe, as the new century approached. Wylie himself, as a civilian, when not in breeches and boots for riding, wore the long trousers and swallow-tail coat then common to most professional men. A portrait of a later date shows him in the uniform of the tsar's army, emblazoned with decorations. His hair, unpowdered, frames a thin, high cheek-boned face in which the dominant feature is a long straight nose. The mouth is sensuous and the eyes, although wide apart, hold a somewhat cynical expression – the whole giving an impression somehow sinister in effect.

A portrait of the tsar himself, painted at about the same time, shows him in a coat embroidered with decorations, tight breeches and knee-length boots. A wide-brimmed hat above his pug-nosed face surmounts a well-curled wig.

Women's fashions were changing too. The Empress Maria Feodorovna clung to the old style, wearing the full-skirted dresses with the low waists which remained popular in Russia, unflattering to the figure though they were. Her daughters-in-law and her daughters, who were old enough to be at court, wore the simple gowns with high waists, now all the rage in London and in Paris where Josephine de Beauharnais, married to the brilliant French general Napoleon Bonaparte, was setting the trend in fashion.

In the following year of 1799, there was much celebration and rejoicing when the Grand Duchess Elizabeth, by now a young woman of twenty, gave birth to a baby girl. Wylie, who was present at the accouchement, may have delivered her himself. Hardly had she been born, however, before tongues started wagging when it was noticed that the child, christened Maria Alexandrovna, was seen to be exceptionally dark whereas both her parents were fair. Rumours circulated that her father was not in fact Alexander but his friend the

Polish Prince Adam Czartoryski, renowned for his powers of seduction. The Grand Duke, however, to whom Czartoryski was 'a man in a million', was delighted with his daughter and both he and his wife were devastated when the little girl died of convulsions when she was only fourteen months old.

Despite attending to the children's ailments, and to those of the tsarina, Maria Feodorovna, now pregnant for the ninth time, Wylie's main concern was the mental state of her husband, the Emperor Paul. By the year 1802 it was obvious, not only to the courtiers and palace staff, but to all with whom he came in contact, that the tsar was suffering from rapidly increasing fits of madness. His mood swings were unpredictable. A favourite one day would be disgraced and sent to Siberia the next. Even old General Suvorov, hero of the war against Turkey, was soon to be treated with a cruelty that seemed insane.

Napoleon Bonaparte was by now advancing across Europe, annexing territory in his path. The Empress Catherine had planned to send an expeditionary force to help the Austrians but Paul, with typical autocracy, had cancelled it. However, in the summer of 1798, as the French seized the island of Malta, headquarters of the Knights of Malta of which Tsar Paul was Grand Master, he decided to join forces with Great Britain and with his former enemy Turkey, in attempting to curb the French advance. Subsequently, when in February 1799 the Second Coalition was formed, Suvorov was recalled to command the combined army of Russia and Austria to fight France in the Italian Peninsula.

Suvorov won a brilliant victory, driving the French from the plains of Lombardy and even threatening Paris as he advanced into the Swiss Alps. Returning to Russia, again a national hero, he expected to be honoured by the tsar. But Paul, both jealous and suspicious, on the excuse that Suvorov had contravened army regulations when appointing his staff, at the last moment cancelled plans for his reception. The old general, ill and tired, died a few months later. He was buried in the crypt of the Nevsky Monastery in St Petersburg, but the tsar, for whom he had won such victories, did not attend the funeral of the man who had served him so well.

Tsar Paul was now so paranoid that he believed the rambling, easily accessible building of the Winter Palace to be a dangerous place for him to live. Despite the sentry boxes, where armed men stood ready to fire at anyone even remotely suspicious who approached, and regardless of the fact that armed bodyguards abounded within the building itself, the tsar was convinced that among them were enemies aiming at his death. Even the sight of army officers chatting harmlessly to each other was transformed in his frenzied mind into a murderous cabal. His fantasies soon increased to the point where he suspected not only the soldiers and courtiers but his own family as well. His wife, Maria Feodorovna, and a former mistress, both totally loyal, came under suspicion, as did his eldest sons and their wives. Alexander, in particular, was forced to deliver his reports twice a day. His fear of his father was so excessive that he could hardly eat or sleep. Watchers saw his hands trembling as he stood before him. At one point his father, having been particularly charming to his son one evening, next morning sent him a message that he should remember the fate of Alexis, whose own father, Peter the Great, had him killed on suspicion of treason.

Yet this strange man, schizophrenic as he plainly was, could still be kind and gentle when pressure was released from his brain.

Obsessed as he was by his delusions, he began building himself a fortress in St Petersburg in 1797. The site he chose was that of the beautiful summer palace of the former Empress Elizabeth, which was summarily pulled down before his own enormous Gothic citadel took its place.

The building, to be known as the Mikhailovsky Palace, was protected by drawbridges and towers where armed men could stand constant guard. Further secluded by moats and drawbridges, there was also a system of underground passages by which, in a case of emergency, Paul believed he could escape. The foundation stone was laid on 8 February 1798, the day that his wife give birth to their ninth and youngest child, named Michael after the saint his father revered. Tsar Paul, having personally inspected the security measures, the water defences, and every single one of the double doors, moved his family, together with his new mistress, Princess Gagarina, into his specially constructed fortress, on 13 February 1801.

By this time it was known throughout Europe that the Tsar was incurably insane. On the rare occasions that he rode through the streets, brandishing a horse whip at any luckless passer-by, people fled in terror at the sight of him. Doctor Rogerson, who had witnessed Tsar Paul's mental deterioration over more than thirty years and was now approaching retirement, wrote, 'Everyone about him is at a loss what to do. Even Kutaisof is becoming very anxious.'[20]

In St Petersburg itself the tension increased but no-one dared to confront him, so great was the terror he inspired. A great admirer of the Consul Bonaparte, as Napoleon then was known, he had so far sent him three personal letters suggesting they should meet to confer on ways to destroy the power of Britain, which he believed to be a menace to unity in Europe. Paul, having already put an embargo on British trade with Russia, and thereby infuriating traders, now proposed to send an army to the Indus as the advance of a combined French and Russian invasion of India.

His army commanders were horrified by the sheer impracticability of such a scheme. There was no way that the soldiers, let alone the horses, could be provisioned over a route into Central Asia, which was still partly unmapped. Paul's own son Constantine declared that now his father had 'declared war on common sense'. More forcefully Nikita Panin, adviser on foreign affairs, told his sovereign quite unequivocally that Russia was totally unprepared for such a war.

It was Panin who first asked the British ambassador, Lord Whitworth, to describe how George III, in his fits of recurring madness, was restrained. Panin, given this information, next conferred in secret with General Pahlen, who as Governor-General of St Petersburg was in constant touch with the Grand Duke Alexander, whom he agreed to approach.

Some two weeks passed before, at the end of February, General Pahlen managed to speak privately with Alexander, putting it to him that his mad father should be deposed and a regency, with himself at its head, established in his place. Alexander, at first horrified, was eventually talked around on the promise that no harm should come to his father, who, he was assured, would be installed in one of the royal palaces near the city, at least until his sanity returned.

CHAPTER SIX

'Uneasy Lies the Head That Wears a Crown'

(Henry IV, Part 2)

On 13 February 1801, Tsar Paul with his wife and his new mistress moved into the Mikhailovsky Palace. Before doing so he personally inspected the fortifications, the moat, the drawbridges, the strong shutters on the windows, the heavily barred double doors. All were secure. Cocooned within his fortress he truly believed he was safe at last.

Once installed himself, he ordered his family to join him. His two eldest sons and their wives moved into their new apartments in the building, which resembled a prison rather than a home.

With them went Wylie, now more than ever indispensible to the tsar, whose suspicion of all around him intensified. As was typical of his unpredictable and idiosyncratic actions Nikita Panin, so recently the tsar's closest advisor but now disgraced for some minor transgression, was sent in exile to the country.

General Pahlen, however, miraculously still in favour, managed to persuade the emperor that Platon Zubov, his grandmother's former lover, and his brothers, together with the Hanoverian mercenary soldier General Bennigsen, should be pardoned for whatever supposed infringements of the law they had committed, and permitted to return to court.

Convinced by now of a conspiracy against him, Paul actually challenged General Pahlen, face to face, demanding that he tell him what he knew. Pahlen, skilfully covering his tracks, admitted that his spies had told him of a conspiracy, but swore he had the situation under very tight control. The traitors would be arrested. There was nothing to fear. The tsar, nonetheless, unconvinced by his assurance, sent urgent word to General Arakcheev – himself banished from court and living on his estate eighty miles away – summoning him to come at once.

It proved a vain attempt at escaping the ever closing trap. Pahlen, rightly guessing what might happen, had the palace gates watched. The despatch rider, arrested, was forced to hand over the tsar's written message, with which Pahlen then confronted Paul, accusing him of perfidy in acting behind his back.

Terrified, the tsar retained the courage to demand that the note be sent. Pahlen, faced with his authority, had no option but to agree, but knowing now that General Arakcheev, although temporarily out of favour, would never, under any circumstances, subscribe to an intrigue to force Paul's abdication, decided to bring forward the planned coup with all possible speed.

Within the city the conspirators met at the house of a Madame Zherebzova, sister of the brothers Zubov. Pahlen, a frequent visitor, saw to it that the police never searched or even watched the house. The Guards regiments, secretly questioned, proved to be loyal to the tsar with the exception of the Semeonovski Regiment, whose officers, declaring themselves to be doubtful of the tsar's sanity, were passionately attached to his son, Grand Duke Alexander.

'The second in command is a sensible quiet young man in whom the crew have confidence,' wrote Count Simon Vorontzov, the Russian ambassador to London, after describing Russia as 'a ship whose captain had gone mad in the midst of a storm'.[21]

Meanwhile the tsar, still convinced he was in imminent danger, continued to cross-question Pahlen, demanding that he tell him if his two elder sons were involved in an intrigue against him. Pahlen assured him, categorically, that they were not, and Paul, although unconvinced of his sincerity, pretended to take him at his word.

Mistrustful of all his family, and believing his friends to be enemies waiting to kill him, Paul now placed his faith in the thick walls and intricate means of defence installed under his own supervision within his new citadel, to save him from all attack.

Pahlen again met the conspirators on Sunday, 22 March. It was agreed that the usual guard should be replaced with men of the Semeonovski Guards and that General Bennigsen, with six of his accomplices, would force their way into the tsar's bedroom at midnight. There they would arrest him and take him across the River Neva to the Fortress of St Peter and St Paul.

Alexander, told next day of what was intended, was apprehensive. Although once more assured of his father's safety, he nonetheless felt instinctively that the plan might well misfire. His nervousness increased as that night he and his brother Constantine, together with their wives, dined with their parents in Mikhailovsky Palace where the newly plastered walls still steamed with the heat of the stoves. Noticing that Alexander was not eating, his father told him that he should see Doctor Wylie, of whose loyalty he still felt confident.

Then, as the dinner ended, the officer of the Guard came in with his nightly report. The tsar is reported to have become almost incoherent with anger as he heard that his regular bodyguard was to be replaced that evening with men of the Semeonovski Regiment, whose officers he did not trust.

Alexander, pleading indigestion, went shortly to his rooms, which were opposite those of his father on the other side of the palace courtyard. How anxiously he must have waited, pacing back and forth across the floor while watching the windows of his father's apartments for any sign of the disturbance that he knew was about to take place.

The night was dark and bitterly cold. The young man watching could not see the officer of the Preobrazhenski Guards who opened the gate of the outer courtyard to admit the cloaked figures of about twenty men. Pahlen headed for Alexander's rooms, but hearing no sound, and believing him to be asleep, did not disturb him. General Bennigsen and Platon Zubov meanwhile went straight for the tsar's apartment. His two valets were overcome and the locked door to the bedroom broken down. In the room, lit by a single candle, there was no sign of the tsar. Then Bennigsen saw a figure crouching, terrified, behind a screen. 'Sire,' he said, 'you have ceased to reign and we are arresting you on the orders of the Tsar Alexander.'[22]

Paul tried to protest. Despite his mental confusion he was still immensely strong and grappled like a demon with the men trying to hold him as he screamed for help. But no one came and one officer, to silence him, hit him on the forehead with a heavy snuff box with a strength that sent him crashing to the floor. Stunned, he lay helpless as another tied a silk scarf round his throat and began to strangle him while a third held a heavy paperweight to his windpipe until the life was choked out of him by force.

The murderers vanished, quickly and silently, through the shattered door of the bedroom and along the passages of the palace into the anonymity of the night.

Behind them they left utter confusion. Servants and aides, alarmed by the terrible noises, rushed to the tsar's room. Wylie, summoned by a near hysterical aide, knew at first glance that he was dead.

Two Scottish compatriots, Doctor Guthrie and Doctor Grieve, were with Wylie when, commanded to sign the death certificate, he stated that the tsar had died of apoplexy. Few people believed it, yet the lie continued to be perpetuated for over 100 years. Doctor Grieve, who helped Wylie to embalm the body, noticed that while there was no evidence of the knife wounds supposedly inflicted by the assassins, there were clear signs of 'a broad contused area round the neck which indicated strangulation'.

Yet the court was said to have been 'very pleased' by Wylie's verdict. Obviously he had been told what to say. But why did he agree to such a deception, which, had it been discovered, could have ruined his professional career?

Clearly the most obvious answer is that he perjured himself to save his life. It is hard to believe that he was actually involved in the conspiracy to kill the tsar, but those who were would not have hesitated to make him the next victim had he exposed their crime.

One man who does cast aspersions, however, is the late-nineteenth-century historian Joyneville who makes the wild – and it would appear totally unfounded – accusation that Wylie was actually among the murderers and that following the tsar's strangulation, he cut his carotid artery to ensure his death.[23] Joyneville gives no sources for his story and contemporary accounts do not even hint at cooperation with the murderers on Wylie's part, other than his signing of the death certificate in compliance with the wishes of the imperial family as. Thus it can only be assumed that it was because he performed the post mortem that, no doubt due to the known jealousy of colleagues, a rumour evolved of his supposed involvement in the crime.

Most importantly, it must be remembered that, in addition to the lack of any written evidence linking Wylie to the assassination of the tsar, it is altogether improbable that Alexander, whose own supposed involvement in his father's death weighed so heavily on his mind, would have placed such implicit trust in Wylie had he, even for one moment, believed him to have been party to the crime. It cannot be denied that thanks to his association with Alexander, and later with Alexander's brother Nicholas who succeeded him as tsar, Wylie, like so many Scots in Russia, did eventually become a rich man. Yet considering the lack of evidence, it should not be imputed that this doctor of reputedly upright character was in any way seduced by gold. It is more likely that, under the circumstances, he had little or no option than to comply with what was demanded of him or else lose his position in the royal household – and with it, most assuredly, his life.

That said, can it be surmised that in falsifying the tsar's death certificate Wylie was acting, at least in part, for altruistic reasons of his own?

It was by then five years since Tsar Paul, ecstatic at Count Kutaisof's apparently miraculous recovery, had made him his personal physician. During that time, in constant attendance, no one had seen more of Paul's decline into madness than had Wylie himself. It therefore seems logical to believe that, recognizing incurable insanity, he thought it better for a man, now dangerous not only to his family but to the millions of people over whom he ruled, to die, if not of natural causes, then by an assassin's hand.

Wylie's lifelong devotion to Alexander – 'My adored Emperor', as he was later to call him – is well known. Watching him grow into manhood, in the years spent in the palace, he had recognized his potential as the leader he was born to be. Now, in this moment of tragedy, dreadful as the circumstances were, he must have recognized the wisdom of the grandmother, the omnipotent Empress Catherine, whose own sudden death had prevented her from naming Alexander as her heir.

CHAPTER SEVEN

Doctor to the New Tsar

On the death of Tsar Paul, James Wylie had already become personal physician to his son, Alexander I, whom he was to serve for twenty-four years. No one knew better than he the agony of mind of the new ruler, who felt himself partly responsible for the death of the father whom he believed he had betrayed. For a short while Wylie feared for Alexander's sanity, as, already in a state of deep depression caused by his guilt, he had then to be told that his eldest sister, Alexandra, who had married the Palatine of Hungary the year before, had died while giving birth to a child.

Wylie now understood that, although not insane like his father, Alexander had the seeds of instability in his mind. He reasoned with him effectively as, refusing to talk to anyone other than his immediate attendants, he kept to his bedroom for some days. This period of intense mental suffering, endured within a darkened room, proved to be the onset of moods of depression which Wylie, through his understanding of them, did his best to assuage.

The one person, apart from his doctor, who helped to maintain Alexander's sanity during those days of torment following his father's death, was his wife Elizabeth. The quiet, fair-haired, almost waif-like figure of the child bride, chosen by his grandmother, to whom he had now been married for eight years, was constantly by his side. While his mother Maria Feodorovna, always a dramatist, had hysterics, and throughout the palace total chaos prevailed, Elizabeth alone remained calm.

It was during this period that Wylie conceived his great respect for her, a feeling perhaps inspired by love. Certain it is that he went to great lengths to protect her by encouraging Alexander to make constant arrangements for her comfort and by making him realize that, with her delicate constitution, she needed a great deal of rest.

Moreover he was soon to be both distressed and angered by the pain inflicted upon her by Alexander's infidelities, which could now no longer be ignored.

Wylie went with Alexander and Elizabeth to Moscow for their coronation in September 1801. The city, founded in 1147, had become in the early fourteenth century the capital of the principality of Slaviansky, when the white-stoned Kremlin was developed into an impregnable fortress. From that time onwards, the many churches crowned with domes and cupolas built in the expanding city had turned the old capital of Russia into a metropolis reminiscent of Rome.

Wylie was among the crowd of enthralled spectators who watched Alexander ride on a white horse from the Petrovsky Palace to the walled citadel of the Kremlin, a distance of four miles. The crowd was ecstatic, calling blessings on the little father, the tall, handsome, fair-haired, blue-eyed prince, so different from the simian-featured Tsar Paul who had died seven months before.

Alexander and Elizabeth remained in Moscow for a month while countless festivities took place. Ball followed ball as the aristocratic ladies of Moscow vied with each other in their efforts to entertain – and in some cases to captivate – the handsome and charming young tsar whose smile was enough to sweep most of them off their feet. Elizabeth soon became exhausted. Never strong, she could not stand the pace at which Alexander plunged so recklessly into anything with which he became involved. Freed at last from the constraint of his grandmother's governance and the terror of his father's regime, it is hardly surprising that, in an age when amorous alliances were considered *de rigueur*, he plunged into the social melee with scarcely an effort at restraint.

It was then that Wylie was to notice how Alexander had an eye for many of the pretty women who virtually fell at his feet. Most were merely flirtations but among them was one more dangerous, a dark-haired, voluptuous Polish beauty, Countess Maria Naryshkin, skilled as a courtesan. She set her cap at Alexander, pursuing him relentlessly, and he, unable to resist the lure of this dominant, sensual woman, succumbed to the attraction of her charms. Shamelessly she revelled in her conquest, flaunting her possession of the man every woman in Moscow wished to seduce, to the chagrin of his young wife.

Standing in the sidelines, Wylie could only watch helplessly the drama that was taking place. Alexander, hopelessly infatuated, was losing control of his senses, regardless, it seems, of the hurt he was causing Elizabeth. There was nothing new in the situation – most men of the aristocracy had mistresses at the time – but to the doctor who now knew them both so well, aware as he was of Elizabeth's love for her husband, and of the instability of Alexander's mind, it was plain that a situation was developing which could result in far-reaching effects on the stability of the Russian hierarchy, if not of the country itself.

Eventually, at the end of October the royal couple left Moscow to return to St Petersburg. Winter was now setting in but Alexander, restless as always, insisted the horses be driven at a furious pace. As the carriage hurtled onwards over metalled roads, while the coach-man lashed the horses to ever greater speed, they passed through dark forests covering much of the distance between the old capital and the new. To Wylie, trundling behind in one of the many coaches carrying equerries, other attendants, and the vast amount of luggage that such an occasion involved, it seemed that the young emperor was possessed by a frantic energy fired by the enormity of his appointed task. Exhausted by the speed and distance of the journey, having barely had time to rest or even wash, Alexander and Elizabeth reached St Petersburg in the space of only five days.

Seen from a distance, the city seemed to rise, almost as if floating, from the marshland on which it was built. In the winter light, as the domes and spires of the many churches shone clear against the sky, it seemed ethereal, divorced from the signs of habitation still remaining out of sight. The stone palaces, the wooden houses, the network of streets and arterial waterways, all might have ceased to exist.

As he approached his capital, Alexander, tireless as he seemed to be, was in fact almost overwhelmed by awareness of the vast responsibility that had been thrust upon his shoulders by his father's death.

CHAPTER EIGHT

The Heavy Clouds of War

Alexander had barely returned to St Petersburg before he received a letter from King Frederick William III of Prussia. He suggested that the two should meet to discuss the affairs of Europe as the threat of the avaricious French First Consul, Napoleon Bonaparte, increased.

In February 1802, Alexander, in reply to yet another missive from Frederick, agreed that a personal discussion would be of much advantage to them both. Although strangers to each other they already had a common bond in that Alexander's second eldest sister Helen, married to Frederick Louis, Prince of Mecklenburg-Schwerin, was a great favourite with both King Frederick and his lovely Queen Louise.

Alexander, accompanied by a train of courtiers – including his doctor James Wylie – arrived at Memel on 10 June.[24] The port, founded by the Knights of the Livonian Order in 1252, defended by a citadel, commands a strong position at the mouth of the River Neman on the shore of the sound of the Memeler Tief, an inlet of the Baltic Sea. Some ninety miles north-east of Königsberg, Memel (now Klaipeda and the most northerly town in Germany) was, then as now, an important port, trading largely in timber, wheat and fish.

For Wylie the town held nostalgia, for sea ports are the same worldwide. Memories of his boyhood came back to him as he saw the masts in the harbour so much like those in Kincardine, whence some of the vessels had probably come. But now it was a harbour with a difference, for men other than seamen swarmed along the crowded quays.

As guests of the king of Prussia, Alexander and the members of his entourage were greatly entertained. Banquets were followed by balls at which Alexander, so strikingly handsome in uniform, danced and flirted with ladies, once again bewitched by his charm. He, for his part, was enchanted with Frederick William's beautiful wife, Princess Louise of Mecklenburg-Strelitz, who was the niece of Queen Charlotte, wife of George III of England. However, whereas her aunt was plain, Louise outshone the court ladies with the gracefulness of her movements and the lustre of her wide-set brown eyes.

Everyone thought she was lovely. Alexander was swept off his feet. Both were young, Louise being just a year older than Alexander, and together they danced in the ballrooms throughout the long summer nights.

In the daytime, however, he discussed politics with her husband. Alexander was willing to support Frederick's authority over the German principalities but the princes themselves, unsure of the worth of the new tsar, were more inclined to deal with Napoleon, now seen as an invincible force.

The Treaty of Amiens, signed between France and Britain in 1802, produced a temperate respite from warfare, which, as most people predicted, was far too good to be true. When war between England and France began again in May 1803, Alexander, although anxious to protect Russian acquisitions in the Mediterranean made by his father during the Second Coalition of 1799, maintained his country's neutrality. But in March 1803 came devastating news. The Duc d'Enghien, a member of the French royal family, had been kidnapped in Baden, home of Alexander's wife Elizabeth, and taken to France, had been tried and executed on the orders of Napoleon himself.

Alexander was horrified, the news that Napoleon had now proclaimed himself Emperor of the French adding to his sense of outrage against what he considered to be regicide. Encouraged by Prince Adam Czartoryski, the Polish nobleman who, formerly his aide, and possibly the lover of his wife, had now become his Deputy Foreign Minister, Alexander formed his Grand Design by which Russia, Austria and Britain would unite against Napoleon, forcing him to abandon his avaricious claims. Accordingly the Third Coalition was finally agreed on 28 July 1805.

By the terms of the treaty Napoleon's empire was to be assaulted by a pincer movement from three sides. The Austrians were to attack southern Germany, supported by a Russian army. The British would send a strong force to the mouth of the River Weser from where, together with Swedish and Russian detachments, they would head through Hanover for the Netherlands. Meanwhile, as Austria attacked Venetia and Lombardy, a joint force of Russian and British soldiers would invade the Kingdom of Naples, whose monarch had pledged his support.

Alexander determined immediately to go with his soldiers. Not even the pleas of Prince Czartoryski would persuade him to change his mind. Wylie would of course go with him. Hastily Wylie assembled his instruments and together with his orderlies packed the bandages, splints and available drugs – mainly laudanum as a painkiller and wine to ease the shock of injury and amputation – into the medical chests which could be carried to the front. All was in readiness when, on the morning of 21 September, after praying for a long time in the cathedral, the tsar led his entourage from St Petersburg to the battlefields ahead.

CHAPTER NINE

Austerlitz

Alexander went first to the Russian part of Poland, which he reached in September. From there he wrote to King Frederick of Prussia asking him to allow Russian troops to pass through his country en route to the Netherlands. Frederick, despite their personal friendship, was unwilling to break his neutrality, and refused. However, when French troops marched through the Prussian enclave of Ansbach to join up with Napoleon's army in Bavaria, he changed his mind. Thus on 21 October 1805, as the British defeated the French and Spanish fleets off Cape Trafalgar, Alexander set off to meet Frederick in Berlin.

James Wylie once more had the chance to witness the reception given by one monarch to another. Bands played, fireworks lit the sky, and banquets and balls were held to entertain the tsar. In the first week of November it was agreed that, should Napoleon fail to consent to the terms of the Third Coalition, Frederick would declare war on France.

There was one informal act to follow, in the form of a personal pledge. On the last night of his visit Alexander, Frederick William and Queen Louise, heavily cloaked against the wind, walked through the streets of the darkened city to the garrison church. There in the candlelit crypt, Frederick William and Alexander leaned forward to embrace each other above the tomb of the Prussian king's ancestor, Frederick the Great. Alexander, who was always emotional, sobbed openly as the two men swore to eternal friendship and to lasting peace between their realms.

On 20 November, Napoleon, who had already taken Vienna and occupied the palace of Schönbrünn, captured Brünn (Brno), the capital of Moravia. The combined forces of Russia and Austria were by then stationed in the small town of Olmutz, about forty miles away from Brünn near the border with Hungary. On 24 November the combined commanders agreed to launch an offensive, aimed at attacking Napoleon at Brünn, before liberating Vienna.

Alexander was now ill, suffering from a bad attack of fever, with Wylie constantly in attendance. As always he proved the worst of patients. Delirious, as his temperature rose, he refused to be bled to reduce the fever or to swallow medicines. Restless as ever, the moment he felt slightly better he tried to leap out of bed, but Wylie restrained him, humouring as a father would a child, a role he increasingly adopted with a man who, while only ten years younger than himself, was nonetheless excitable as a young and petulant boy. Recovering, but still so weak that he actually submitted to Wylie's advice, he proceeded by coach, rather than on horseback, to the town of Wischau (Vykov) twenty miles to the south. Here he received an emissary from Napoleon, who could not have been worse chosen, proving to be General Savary, formerly chief of the gendarmerie who had been instrumental in kidnapping the Duc d'Enghien prior to his execution. Savary brought a message from Napoleon asking for a meeting to discuss terms of peace with Alexander.

Incapacitated as he was at that moment, suffering from a return of the fever, Alexander sent his own envoy in return in the form of Prince Peter Dolgoruky who, considering Napoleon to be an upstart wearing a dirty shirt, affronted him to his face. Napoleon, for his part, called the Russian prince 'a perfumed booby',[25] and went back in anger to his headquarters near Brünn.

The weather was now very cold, the icebound roads pot-holed and dangerous. Alexander's favourite chestnut mare stumbled and came down on her knees, giving him a heavy fall. Two days later, still badly bruised, he rode to a nearby village to meet the Emperor Francis of Austria.

Napoleon had by now retreated to within a few miles of Brünn. Military genius that he was, having guessed at his enemy's intention, he had chosen his position expressly to entice Prince Mikhail Kutuzov, the Russian commander, to outflank him in an attempt to cut off his line of retreat to Vienna.

The two armies were so close that on the still, moonlit night of 1 December, they could see each other's camp fires. At three o'clock in the morning, Alexander was woken by his anxious staff as commotion broke out in the French camp. But it proved to be only the soldiers cheering their emperor on the anniversary of his coronation, an event they believed to be a lucky sign.

As dawn broke a fog descended, making the enemy invisible to the Russian soldiers, who, as Napoleon had predicted, advanced on his right flank. They broke through and, again in accordance with Napoleon's plans, were surrounded and disseminated by heavy artillery.

Suddenly, as the sun dispersed the mist, Marshal Soult's cavalry bore down on the centre of the allied line. The two emperors, Alexander and Francis, watching from a knoll, came under fire. Amid much confusion and cries for their safety they left their vantage point. The fighting then continued until, at about midday, the tsar's brother Constantine led the Imperial Guard into a heroic counter-attack.

Napoleon himself was watching as over 1,000 horsemen galloped up the slope of the Pratzen Plateau into the mouths of his waiting guns. 'There are many fine ladies who will weep tomorrow in Petersburg,' he said as he saw the dreadful result.[26]

The battle of Austerlitz – claimed both then and thereafter as the French emperor's greatest victory – was over. 'Roll up the map of Europe. It will not be needed hereafter', was the verdict of William Pitt.

Alexander, mentally and physically exhausted, his mind numbed by incomprehension of the horrors he had witnessed during the course of that day, was on the verge of collapse. Nonetheless, hearing that Emperor Francis was at the small town of Czeitsch, some eight miles away, he insisted on riding there immediately. The short December day was ending, and in near darkness, at a small village on the way, he collapsed, falling forwards on the neck of his horse. Wylie, with him as ever, managed, with the help of the guards who formed his escort, to lift him from the saddle and to carry him into a hut where all he could find to cover his shivering body was a peasant's straw-filled quilt. He had no medicines with him, not even quinine.

The night hours seemed endless to Wylie as he sat, fighting off his

45

own longing for sleep, by the side of the restless, desperately ill tsar. The crisis came at three o'clock in the morning when Alexander screamed in agony, sobbing with the pain of violent cramp. Quite unable to help him, Wylie asked Prince Adam Czartoryski to stay with him before stumbling out into the night to shout for his horse. Once astride, by the wavering light of a lantern, he managed to make the animal pick its way over the rough road, churned up by many vehicles into frozen ruts, over the four miles or so to the small town of Czeitsch, headquarters of Emperor Francis.

Dismounting, he somehow gained entry into one of the houses requisitioned for the occupation of the emperor's staff, where he begged an Austrian officer to let him have some red wine. Amazingly, the man refused. Wylie, incensed at such inhumanity and well known for speaking his mind, must at this point have let fly, doubtless telling him what he thought of him in the language of the Kincardine docks. Somehow he got past him into the interior of the house where he found a servant who, either by bribery or intimidation, he forced into giving him a little rough red wine.

It proved effective. Or, more probably, Alexander's strong constitution brought him back to life. By morning, now fit enough to ride, he joined the long-faced, frigid Emperor Francis and the portly, one-eyed Russian General Kutuzov at Czeitsch.

Although told of the dreadful casualties (25,000 to 30,000 soldiers of the allied armies had been killed) Alexander remained determined to pursue the campaign. Convinced that Frederick William of Prussia would honour their agreement by bringing his army into the field, he assured the Austrian emperor that Napoleon could be defeated in a renewed assault. However, Francis, mistrustful of Frederick William, refused to believe that any such hope remained. Subsequently, on the following day, 4 December 1805, a treaty of peace between France and Austria was arranged. Included was the term that the Russians must also capitulate and withdraw immediately from Moravia to return within the frontier of their own land.

CHAPTER TEN

The Fourth Coalition

Alexander returned to St Petersburg to a rapturous reception from his people. Their little father was back and with the defeat of Austerlitz still unknown to most of them, he was still their hero.

Only his wife, Elizabeth, his doctor and, to some extent his mother, Maria Feodorovna, knew of his mental agony as the images of those dreadful scenes of battle, and of what he now felt to be his own inadequacy as a commander, tortured his sensitive mind. Wylie, for his part, cursed his own failure to relieve the misery he found himself forced to witness. Medicine, even if forced on Alexander, would be useless and other remedies there were none. Sympathy and exhortation to try to put his troubles from his mind produced only outbursts of fury for which he invariably apologized with all of his endearing charm. Eventually, and as his doctor now knew inevitably, Alexander found some comfort in the arms of his Polish mistress, the vibrant, dark-haired Maria Naryshkina.

Elizabeth, now largely estranged from Alexander, chose to ignore the reincarnation of this love affair, which she was powerless to prevent. Perhaps, like Wylie, she was grateful for anything that would lift him from the black cloud of misery which appeared to monopolize his mind. Resigned by now to his unfaithfulness, she had long become accustomed to his insatiable roving eye. Handsome and enormously attractive himself, he loved both the admiration and the company of pretty women. Foremost among them was the acknowledged beauty the Prussian Queen Louise, whose image in flickering candlelight lingered obsessively in his memory.

It was on his return to Russia that the Emperor Alexander, the welfare of his soldiers lying heavily on his mind, ordered Wylie 'to make out preventative and curative instructions for the Russian troops in Corfu and the other Greek islands threatened from their "situation" with yellow fever or the new American plague.'[27] The result was Wylie's book, *On the Yellow American Fever*. Dedicated to Alexander and printed in Russian, by the Medical Press at St Petersburg in 1805, it provides a short historical account, followed by a comprehensive discussion on the disease, with clear recommendations for its prevention and treatment.

By then he must have already been working on his famous handbook on surgical operations, again written in Russian and the first to be printed in that language, which was published in 1806.

James Wylie was also appointed Inspector-General of the Russian army board of health in 1806, a post he was to hold for nearly fifty years until 1854. In that same year, as the Fourth Coalition between Prussia, Russia, Saxony, Sweden and Britain was formed, at the request of King Frederick William, he was seconded as adviser to the Prussian medical staff.

The commander-in-chief of the Prussian army was the Duke of Brunswick, Prince Friedrich Ludwig of Hohenlohe commanding the left wing. However, with little communication between the military leaders, the two parts of the Prussian army failed to co-operate successfully in a co-ordinated campaign.

The town of Jena lies on the plateau west of the River Saale in today's eastern Germany. It was here, on the evening of 14 October 1806, that Hohenlohe's force of 38,000 – mostly newly conscripted men – was confronted by part of the French army under the command of Marshal Lannes.

Jean Lannes, a strikingly handsome man, born the son of a blacksmith, had risen high in Napoleon's estimation during previous campaigns. Realizing he was outnumbered, he immediately sent urgent requests for reinforcements. During the night new units joined him until, by the morning, he had approximately 50,000 men with the assurance that more were approaching.

Knowing that he had the advantage of numbers, Lannes forced the Prussians onto open ground, where the cavalry could be most effectively employed. Hohenlohe, seeing his men mown down as Marshal Ney launched an attack, also desperately appealed for reinforcements. At one o'clock Napoleon ordered a general advance, and after two hours of deadly struggle, the Prussians were over-powered. Many were cut down by the sabres of the French cavalry as they tried to flee. While the French lost only 5,000 of their seasoned troops, an estimated 25,000 of the young, untried Prussian soldiers are said to have been killed.

Further north at Auerstadt, both Marshal Davout and the Swedish Marshal Bernadotte, were ordered to reinforce Napoleon's army. Davout, Napoleon's youngest marshal, marched south from Eckarts-berg, where he had just fought a battle with the Prussians in which Prince Henry of Prussia had been wounded. The Prussians failed to block his advance through the Kösen Pass and Davout ordered Major General Gudin to attack the village of Hassenhausen.

Gudin met fierce resistance and shortly before ten o'clock the Duke of Brunswick ordered a full assault on Hassenhausen. Within minutes the Prussian Commander-in-Chief was carried mortally wounded from the field. The Prussian command was in confusion and Davout, seeing what was happening, ordered a counter-attack. Within an hour the battle was over and King Frederick William, defeated, ordered his troops to withdraw.

From Wittenburg, on 20 October, Davout wrote to the Prince of Neufchatel, Major General of the Grand Army, to tell him that the advance guard of the Third Corps had crossed the Elbe and entered Wittenburg. The Prussians had tried, but failed, to set fire to the bridge as they retreated.

Wylie, as a regimental surgeon both during and after the battle, must have worked ceaselessly, carrying out operations – largely amputations – and dressing wounds. Again, as at Austerlitz, he was to witness the frightful suffering of the wounded Prussian soldiers, to whom, except for the officers, no medical attention was given. Left to lie in the blood-soaked, churned-up mud of the field in which they had fought, there was little or no hope for any of them to survive. It was truly claimed that a cannon ball was the soldier's greatest friend. Killed instantly, he would be spared a night of torture before the inevitable end.

The French, on the other hand, had ambulances, which carried men to the dressing stations adjacent to the battlefield itself. Wylie, horrified by what he knew to be an unnecessary loss of life, was already laying plans for similar arrangements which he knew could save many wounded men.

Aware as he was that Alexander's despondency after Austerlitz had been largely induced by the awful sights of the battlefield, Wylie now felt confident that the moment had come to put forward his case for adopting modern methods of improving the medical services of the Russian army. Subsequently, on returning to St Petersburg, Alexander, as Wylie had anticipated, gave his full attention to his plans. There was, as he rightly insisted, no time for delay. Renewal of the war with Napoleon now seemed inevitable and Alexander, again as Wylie had rightly guessed, seized enthusiastically on his suggestions of erecting field hospitals, at which not only officers, but men of all ranks could be attended to. Unaware of – or perhaps oblivious to – the fact that the friend and physician whose attempts at calming his recent despair had been so brusquely refused was now twisting his arm, he set his seal on what was asked for with all the enthusiasm which Wylie, only so recently, had believed he might never see again.

Speed was indeed essential, for even as Wylie gave orders for the field hospitals to be assembled, news came from Prussia that, with their army virtually obliterated, King Frederick William and Queen Louise had fled to Königsberg in the extreme north-east of their kingdom. Behind them they left their capital to be occupied by the now apparently invincible Emperor of the French.

On 25 October the French army entered Berlin. On reaching the city, Napoleon immediately gave orders for the Charlottenburg Palace to be searched from the attics to the vaults. The discovery of letters from Alexander proved that he had been urging Frederick William to continue his war against Napoleon even as the peace treaty between them was in the process of being arranged. Napoleon, furiously angry, was then handed a portrait of Alexander, found in the queen's bedroom, together with letters from him to her, written in undeniably affectionate terms. Spitefully he broadcast the correspondence, inserting innuendos in official bulletins, to the detriment of Louise's reputation and to the ridicule of the tsar.

In November 1806, as churches throughout Russia denounced the French emperor as the Antichrist, the enemy of mankind, Napoleon entered Warsaw and annexed the part of Poland held by Austria.

Subsequently General Bennigsen, in command of the Russian army, halted the apparently invincible French advance in the inconclusive battle near the Prussian town of Eylau on 7 February the following year.

Again, as at Austerlitz, there was appalling loss of life. Heavy snow had fallen, and men died of hypothermia as much as from the murder of the guns. The first field hospitals, although primitive in their inception, were soon to be introduced.

In March Alexander, with Wylie as usual in attendance, drove at his accustomed speed to Memel where, once again, he met Frederick William and Louise. This time, however, there were no balls and banquets. Frederick William was sunk in depression and Louise's lovely face was drawn and lined with the sorrow and anxiety they had both endured. Leaving Memel the two monarchs travelled to the battle zone where, at Bartenstein, Alexander assured Frederick that he would uphold his claim to former frontiers in any dealings with the French.

It was, as Alexander knew, an empty promise. The French now held all of Prussia except Königsburg and still their conquering army advanced. Tension increased in St Petersburg as the threat of invasion to Russia itself became acute. On 14 June the tsar's army of 61,000 men, commanded by General Bennigsen, confronted what he at first believed to be a small force near the town of Friedland on the River Alle. The Russian army, divided by the swift-flowing stream, was overcome by a French force, 80,000 strong, which, under Napoleon's own command, completely defeated the Russians within a space of three hours.

Again the casualties were heavy: 12,000 on the French side, 20,000 on the Russian. The French had already established field hospitals. Baron Larrey, Napoleon's Surgeon-General, was the inventor of the light, two-wheeled ambulances, the *ambulances volantes*, which bore wounded men swiftly to the surgeon's tents. And now, for the first time, thanks to the Scottish surgeon Wylie's sway over their tsar, the wounded Russian soldiers were also carried to emergency medical stations near the battlefield for treatment, where previously they would have been left to die.

Was Wylie himself there to witness the triumph of his persistence?

The question at once springs to mind. But unfortunately, as with so much else about him, this is something we shall never know. Records do not mention his presence on the battlefield and it seems more likely that he was with Alexander at Tilsit on the Niemen, some seventy miles from Friedland, where it is known that news first reached him of his army's devastating defeat.

Despairing, the tsar then realized the futility of continuing a war that was proving so utterly ruinous in terms of both money and lives.

CHAPTER ELEVEN

Tilsit

On the morning of 25 June 1807, at eleven o'clock, the Emperor Alexander reached the east bank of the River Niemen, which at that point was as wide as the Seine. With him were his brother, the snub-nosed Constantine, and the morose King Frederick William of Prussia, on whose land they actually stood. Both banks of the river were lined with spectators, who gazed in fascination at the large raft, towed out earlier into mid-stream, shining resplendent in the sun. On board was a pavilion with monograms of the letter A facing the right bank and N the left.

For two hours Alexander waited in a village inn. Wylie, in attendance, noticed his agitation, the restless movements, the height-ened colour of his face, the snapping of his fingers in frustration at the waste of time. Noon passed and he was all but screaming with impatience when, at about one o'clock, his ADC Count Paul Lieven heard cheering from the far side of the river and at last the squat, blue-coated figure of Napoleon, astride his beautiful Arab stallion Marengo, was seen riding down to the west bank where a boat lay waiting to carry him out to the raft.

Alexander and his retinue at once boarded the ferry, which took them out to the raft where Napoleon was now aboard. As the two emperors shook hands, onlookers saw how Alexander towered above Napoleon, making him seem even more diminutive. Did they, one wonders, also notice the tall dark Scotsman, standing as usual to one side? If within earshot, he can hardly have relished the opening exchange of words.

'Sire, I hate the English no less than you do and I am ready to assist you in any enterprise against them,' was Alexander's greeting, to which Napoleon quickly replied, 'In that case everything can be speedily settled between us and peace is made.'

The two men emerged smiling after talking for nearly two hours.

The next day they met again on the raft and for a week thereafter they wined and dined with each other and rode throughout the surrounding country. Sometimes Frederick William accompanied them but Napoleon had little respect for him, calling him 'a nasty king'[28] and Queen Louise, who arrived at Tilsit on 6 July, accused Alexander of deceiving her and betraying her country to Bonaparte. Later, however, on the next day, when the formal treaty was signed, it was found that two thirds of her husband's territory was to be restored to him at the special request of the tsar.

Alexander having acquiesced to Napoleon's request that he should pressurize Denmark and Sweden to join Napoleon's economic system, if necessary by force of arms, then in open aggression, agreed to cancel all trade with Britain and to order her government to surrender her colonies under a threat of war.

He had turned his doctor into an enemy! Wylie, like the many other Scots and English in Russia, was a native of the country with which it was now at war. Doubtless he himself considered his new status to be nothing more than a technicality, as, it would appear, did Alexander. Nonetheless, it gave impetus to his Russian confederates to cast yet further aspersions on the man whose success and influence is known to have caused jealousy throughout his career.

Invidious as was his own position, Wylie, through his proximity to the tsar, must have known that despite their outward cordiality Alexander was undeceived as to the French emperor's intentions. The two had spent long hours studying maps while Napoleon explained the frontiers of the Europe he envisaged, while at the same time it had been obvious that from the Prussian part of Poland, now as a French protectorate renamed the Grand Duchy of Warsaw, war against Russia could swiftly be renewed.

'*Dieu nous a sauvé*,' he wrote to his favourite sister Catherine.[29]

She replied with a verbal bombardment. 'While I live I shall not get used to the idea of knowing that you pass your days with Bonaparte . . . for the man is a blend of cunning, ambition and pretence.'

More clearly than her brother, she saw that by pledging Russia to Napoleon's Continental System, he had made a gross mistake. A breach with Britain and a war in the Baltic would have a drastic effect on Russian trade. The country would face bankruptcy.

'We shall have made huge sacrifices and for what?' his sister demanded to know.

Once returned to his capital the tsar, at Wylie's instigation, began visiting the hospitals in St Petersburg that had been founded by his grandmother Catherine. Sometimes he gave prior warning so that dignitaries, in their finery, waited his approach. More often, to catch them unawares, he arrived completely unannounced.

In the May of that year of 1808, both Alexander and his wife Elizabeth endured a personal tragedy which drove them near to despair. Already they had lost their eldest daughter as a baby. Now, suddenly, their second child, a little girl they had called Lisinka, died of convulsions brought on by teething, in her mother's arms.

Her parents were inconsolable. Wylie, trying to offer sympathy, told Alexander that there was absolutely no reason why he and Elizabeth should not have other healthy children who would survive.

'No, my friend. God does not love my offspring,' was the tsar's sad reply.

Wylie was now to witness how the loss of their child, which might have united them, instead drew the royal couple still further apart. Elizabeth remained in mourning for two years while Alexander returned to his Polish mistress, Maria Naryshkina.

Again, in this relationship, misfortune seemed to haunt him. Of the three children she bore him, all of them girls, only one survived. Despite Wylie's assurance that this was through no fault of his own, Alexander was thrown into deep despondency, believing that his progeny were cursed.

CHAPTER TWELVE

Head of the Russian Military Medical Services

The year 1808 was to prove a landmark for Wylie, for at this time he first published his famous Russian military pharmacopoeia, the *Pharmacopoeia castrensis Ruthena*, on which he had been working over the last three years. While providing a full coverage of pharmacy and pharmacognosy, it also included the new pharmaceutical nomenclature. Known as *Pharmacopoeia castrensis Wylie*, it ran through four editions and was replaced only twelve years after his death, in 1866. Other publications of Wylie's included the first Russian medical manual for in-field use and the translation of a book by James Johnson about the influence of hot climate on health.

It was in January 1808 that Wylie became President of the Medical Chirurgical Academy, a post he was to hold for twenty years. As such he was placed in charge of the Academy established by a decree of Tsar Paul, when it had been realized that the few medico-chirurgical schools in St Petersburg, Moscow, Kronstadt and Elizavetgrad were unable to keep pace with the demand for doctors, especially in the army and navy.

Primarily the academy was intended to become a central educational institution for military surgeons and to have sufficient capacity to offer standards of teaching comparable to the state of science abroad. Opened in 1800, it developed into a highly significant medical school in Russia and in the present day, as the Military Medical Academy in St Petersburg, it remains prestigious.

Initially there were many problems of organization to be overcome as the Academy was placed under the control of the newly created Ministry of Internal Affairs. Also the vast influx of students from the now dissolved Moscow Medico-Chirurgical Academy and the merger with the Medico-Chirurgical Kalinkin Institute, meant that both management and training had to be based on improvised instructions only. Legal regulations, comprising the foundations of the Academy, were later adopted in 1808.

Starting in 1805, a search was put in motion for a specialist who could be recognized internationally as being capable of developing a plan of reform which would establish the Academy as being among the best medical schools in Europe. The choice finally fell on Johann Peter Frank, renowned as a clinician, as the creator of the 'medical police' and as a public health care organizer. Already connected with reforms of medical education in Pavia, Vienna and Vilna, Frank was invited to come from that city to St Petersburg to become Surgeon in Ordinary and rector of the Academy. By the end of 1806 he had submitted his comprehensive reform plan to the Minister of Internal Affairs, Count Kochubei. The document was reviewed by Alexander Crichton, General Staff Doctor for Civilian Healthcare, James Wylie, the Surgeon in Ordinary, and Count Zavadovsky, the Minister of Public Education. Frank's plan was expressly geared to the needs of the army and the military character of the Academy. He did not want, however, to create a mere 'vocational' school for military medicine, but a true higher school with a weighty scientific reputation. In spite of some major alterations and high costs, his proposal was accepted and adopted as the Academy's new regulations.

Wylie, like a cat watching its prey, was waiting to pounce. Frank had endangered his own plans. Asked to review the reform projects, he produced several critical appraisals of all that he had suggested. He then drew up an alternative proposal, which the emperor immediately sanctioned. Thus, two days after the publication of the Regulations, Alexander, to everyone's confusion and disappointment, declared it invalid 'due to expected changes based on some reasons produced by the Surgeon in Ordinary Wylie'.

Frank, mortified and declaring himself 'ambushed', did keep his post of lecturer and rector before returning to Vienna in March 1808. Conveniently, and perhaps tactfully, he left just before, after two years of deliberations, Wylie's Regulations were approved on 28 July 1808.

Frank did have cause to feel injured but nonetheless Wylie's plan was superior to his in terms of Russia's urgent needs. His draft does not bear the touch of a scholar but evinces the confident tone of a military and practical man. Wylie's strict and succinct concept worked better in the time of constant devastating wars when the country required a reliable institution to provide the army and navy with doctors who would have received at least standard training and, more importantly, would be familiar with field surgery. This plan was also well suited to the Russian mentality.

The provisions of the Regulations should be discussed from this point of view. The mission and structure of the Academy were conceived on a grand scale; quite appropriately, maintenance, according to Wylie, should cost 386,000 roubles per year whereas Frank suggested 'only' 170,000. As well as human medicine, departments for veterinary medicine and pharmacy were also to be set up.

Most importantly, at least as far as the ordinary man was concerned, Wylie insisted that all lectures were to be given in Russian instead of the scholarly Latin, as had hitherto been used. In doing so he took into account the current needs, in particular the awakening nationalist tendencies in Russia. Management of the Academy began more and more to resemble military discipline. It was no longer headed by a rector but by a president with wide-ranging powers, who would be supported by a vice-president in charge of the Moscow branch, an academic secretary, and a managing director. As president, James Wylie (appointed three days after the approval of the Regulations, on 1 August 1808) also became the Chief Inspector of Army Healthcare, emphasizing the military nature of the institution founded by the Ministry of Internal Affairs.

The faculty consisted of twenty-four full professors and twenty-four assistant professors. The studies were controlled by the 'conference' chaired by the president and composed of full academic members, i.e. professors and secretariat. The assistant professors attended the conferences without a right to vote. The applicants for full professorship had to deliver a test lecture in front of the conference; assistant professors also had to pass a written and oral examination before the test lecture. The professors had to submit the books on which they based their teaching for the conference's approval to allow changes to be made in their own books. The Regulations no longer mentioned professors' rights, as had Frank's document, but only responsibilities, obedience coming to the foreground.

The remaining fourteen sections of the Regulations dealt with the rights of the Academy, given the 'imperial' title immediately, the business management, the three departments, the students, the curriculum, the examinations and the academic degrees. With these Regulations, the institution acquired foundations for its work which remained valid until the end of the nineteenth century with relatively few changes.

Due to his attendance on the emperor, Wylie could only seldom perform the office of the 'conference' chairman. Nevertheless he was informed in detail about all the proceedings at the institution and reserved his final word even for minor issues, insofar as teaching, the faculty and the students were concerned. He cared less about the economy, so much so that the first years of his office witnessed some serious irregularities in the Academy's housekeeping. In most cases Wylie treated members of the 'conference' in a considerate manner. He supported all professors and students who distinguished them- selves with special achievements and diligence. The best graduates of the Academy were allowed to choose jobs by themselves: the way to privileged guards troops was open to them, or they would receive bursaries to travel abroad.

As president, Wylie worked tirelessly for the Academy. He saw that the authority of the medical profession could be enhanced only by broadening and improving education, especially for military sur- geons.

Wylie made sweeping reforms. He tried to improve the academic and legal status as well as the authority of the military surgeon. In addition he issued many important directives concerning the care of the wounded in war, organization of hospitals, recruitment and disablement of soldiers, essential surgical operations and the order and cleanliness of hospitals.[30]

Now given a free hand he showed his real genius for administra- tion, reforming – and in many cases creating – army medicine.

Methods of treatment in the hospitals of the early nineteenth century have been described as a cross between learning and witch- craft. The medical treatment of patients was most severely limited, both by the lack of accurate knowledge of the actual cause of disease, and because of the lack of almost all the effective drugs known to us today. Certainly Wylie was advanced by the standards of his time.

Descriptions of his insistence on ventilation and cleanliness and of space between patients' beds show that he was aware of the dangers of infection through contagion, although obviously not from the still undiscovered existence of germs. Nonetheless the importance of diet was recognized, as was 'the goodness of the air'.

Much reliance was placed on the treatment known as 'salivations of mercury' for which special warm rooms were provided. The treatment was unpleasant, with mercury being administered until symptoms of poisoning occurred. Absorption of the element, when applied as an ointment to the skin, was more rapid when the skin was warm, hence the need for heated rooms. Increased secretion of saliva was produced, two to three pints a day being thought ideal. But this often resulted in side-effects such as ulcers on the tongue and in the mouth, loss of weight, weakness and tremor. Nevertheless, despite the pain and disorientation endured by the sufferers, it was firmly believed that the evil tumours of the disease were excreted in the saliva, and so (at least in some instances) a cure was achieved. A hundred years were to pass before this plainly barbaric treatment was used only for the treatment of syphilis, in which it seems to have had some effect.[31]

Nitric acid was also much used, both as a tonic and a means of subduing stomach upsets. Although in its natural form a deadly poison, when greatly diluted with water to the proportion of one fluid ounce of the strong acid to nine fluid ounces of distilled water, it was safe enough that when sweetened with syrup it formed 'an agreeable potion, which was seldom objected to by the patients'. Nitric acid was also used extensively in the treatment of purpura (blood vessels bursting to form purple bruises, as its name implies), for application to ulcers and even as a gargle in cases of tonsillitis, in which it was especially helpful.

Muriatic or hydrochloric acid was also used as a common palliative, especially in cases of typhus fever, then so common among soldiers living in close proximity. Described as 'a powerful tonic' and also as 'an excellent application to the gangrenous ulcers', it too was used as a gargle when combined with tincture of capsicum in infusion of roses.[32]

Doctor Rogerson's panacea, in addition to laxatives, was 'James's Powders', the nostrum employed by all English doctors of the period,

as well as Wylie, we can presume. In addition he relied upon
bleeding, then the most widely used form of medical treatment, in
Russia as throughout the world. Because it reduces the temperature,
bloodletting was one of the oldest therapeutic manoeuvres known to
medicine. Originally this involved opening a vein in the cubital fossa
and allowing the blood to run into a bleeding bowl. Then, over the
course of the seventeenth, eighteenth and nineteenth centuries, a
technique was refined which involved the use of cupping glasses. The
glasses were warmed before being applied to the patient's skin, where
they became firmly attached because of the partial vacuum created as
the air inside the glass cooled. Blood was thus dawn to the patient's
skin for the treatment to begin. The scarificator is a metal instrument
punctuated with a series of slots through which project several metal
blades which cut the skin to a depth determined by a screw mechan-
ism. The lancets were discharged by a trigger and the blood drained
into a bowl. Although it may sound barbaric, the technique was not
considered painful and anaesthetics, even when later invented, were
very seldom used.

CHAPTER THIRTEEN

'Napoleon Thinks I Am No Better Than a Fool'
(Alexander to his sister Catherine Pavlovna, 8 October 1808)

Despite his personal sadness the tsar was soon forced back into the
political arena as news came of the French Emperor Napoleon's
invasion of both Portugal and Spain. At once it became obvious that
as troops were withdrawn from the Grand Duchy of Warsaw, he was
now more than ever dependent upon Russian support to prevent
renewed war with Austria.

In the last week of August 1808, swinging from apathy to action as
was typical of his volatile nature, Alexander wrote to the French
emperor telling him that he hoped to meet him in Erfurt, a small town
in Thuringia, where they might again confer as they had at Tilsit the
previous year.

Then with accustomed impetuosity, he was off once more, racing
at breakneck speed in a *caleche* (light carriage) for a distance of 750
miles. Again there was joyous celebration as the two emperors rode
into the town together among peeling bells and cheering crowds.

For a week they discussed politics, but by now the former camaraderie
was beginning to wear thin. Each became increasingly suspicious of the
other and Alexander, writing to his favourite sister Catherine, told her
that he now thought it obvious that Napoleon thought him a fool.

The main source of their controversy was Napoleon's attitude to
the Austrians. Alexander wanted to confer with them, particularly on
the subject of the Continental System whereby Napoleon planned to
enforce an embargo on British trade. Desperate to return to the Iberian
Peninsula, infuriated by such prevarication, the emperor threw his
hat on the ground and stamped on it in uncontrollable rage. Later he
complained to General Caulaincourt, his newly appointed ambassador to St Petersburg, that Alexander was as stubborn as a mule.

Eventually, however, despite the disagreements, a secret treaty was signed. By its terms the two emperors reaffirmed their alliance, and in view of the very real necessity for trade, resolved to approach George III of England with offers of peace. Finland and the provinces of Moldavia and Wallachia were to be acceded to Russia, although it was stated specifically that the province of Holstein-Oldenburg should not be annexed. Also it was conceded that all the Turkish lands, apart from areas around the Danube, were to remain under the sultan's rule.

Official business concluded, Napoleon approached Alexander on the delicate subject of his marriage. Josephine was childless and he was planning to divorce her, being desperate for an heir. Suggestions had already been put forward to Alexander, via his ambassador, Count Armand de Caulaincourt, that his sister Catherine might be a suitable bride. Alexander, however, was revolted by the idea. Katya, as her family called her, was only twenty while Napoleon was twice her age. But this was the least of the reasons why the thought of his favourite sister being used as a political pawn as a wife for the self-made Emperor of France was something he could not entertain. Through words couched in diplomacy, Napoleon got the message that under no circumstances whatever would Alexander, whom he thought he held in his thrall, even countenance the idea of his marriage to either Catherine, or his youngest sister Anna. He did not receive it kindly. Never could Napoleon Bonaparte accept an insult to his pride. When they parted onlookers noted the French emperor's mood to be grim.

Meanwhile, Alexander's own marriage now seemed likely to fall apart. At the end of 1810 de Maistre, the Sardinian minister at the Russian Court, writing to Victor-Emanuel, the King of Naples, told him that the estrangement between the emperor and empress had now reached a state of impasse. Elizabeth had shown great dignity in turning a blind eye to her husband's dalliances. His long-lasting affair with Maria Naryshkin, who had openly flaunted her pregnancies, had proved particularly hurtful to Elizabeth, but goaded as she was by this woman, to whom her mother-in-law showed great favour, Elizabeth forgave Alexander, whom she still slavishly adored.

Some time after Alexander's return from Erfurt, however, when Elizabeth learned that a suite of rooms in the Winter Palace was being prepared for some woman, she succumbed to both anger and grief. The lady's identity has never been identified: it may have been Naryshkina or a new mistress, whom Tolstoy mentions, although he does not give her name. Whoever it was, the insult of her husband's mistress moving into the Winter Palace was more than Elizabeth could bear. She told her sister Amelia, who was living with her, that she could not stay under the same roof with any mistress and would return to Baden forthwith.

The domestic crisis of the emperor and empress transfixed the gossipmongers of St Petersburg. For a short time, all talk of threatened war was forgotten. Amelia wrote at once to their mother, who in turn sent a letter to Elizabeth, begging her to change her decision. Alexander, suddenly aware, it would seem for the first time, how greatly Elizabeth was distressed, suddenly came to his senses as he realized that he was about to lose the one woman he really loved, despite his many infidelities. Shocked into contrition, he begged her to forgive him. The workmen departed from the Winter Palace and the royal marriage, at least on the face of it, somehow continued to survive.

Wylie worked to improve the running of the army hospitals with a speed spurred on by the knowledge that war was about to be declared. Committed as he was to this project, his task was not made easier by the fact that as personal doctor to the imperial family he was ever at the beck and call of the tsar.

Alexander's loathing of the tyranny of serfdom was by now well known. Although some landlords were benevolent, others were quite the reverse. No one was more aware of this than Wylie, as the following incident must prove.

Told of the appalling treatment that a certain aristocratic lady, who lived some way from Moscow, was meting out to her serfs, Alexander sent Wylie, dragging him from his most important work, to examine the condition of the peasants living on her land. Directed to act as he thought best, Wylie, after an inspection, was so horrified by what he found that he sent flour, meat and wine over a distance of 200 versts[33] for the relief of the starving people for which the virago who was so maltreating them was forced to pay.

Alexander's wish to abolish serfdom was by now well known. It was also common knowledge that, in view of what was seen to be a coming time of national crisis as Napoleon threatened war, and reliant as he was on the landlords for support, his aim was unlikely to succeed.

Foremost among the tsar's advisors on his plans to give the mass of his people at least a voice of their own was Mikhail Speransky, the man who had now become the tsar's private secretary. Speransky, the son of a village priest, had trained originally for the priesthood, then became a civil servant and, noted for his diligence and comprehension of finance, had gradually risen to be head of the Second Department in the Ministry of Interior.

The tsar, having recognized his competence, had requested his release from this employment to become his personal assistant. In doing so he must have known that Speransky was an admirer of the new regime in France, but plainly was unaware that Napoleon planned to exploit his known influence over the tsar.

Speransky returned from Erfurt to be made both State Secretary and Assistant Minister of Justice. As such, with Alexander he planned to make sweeping government reforms. Although supreme power would remain with the tsar and a Council of State, the people would have a voice through elected representative assemblies. He also proposed that the taxation system should be based on the agricultural wealth of the country, an idea much resented by the landlords, whose money came largely from their land.

Most dramatically Alexander supported Speransky's decision to abolish the privileges which allowed the advancement of the aristocracy in the civil service. Still more drastically, he allowed him to enforce the applicants for these positions to take a written examination.

The resulting outrage was predictable. Many of the nobility were incapable of passing a test in mathematics set in Russian, let alone in the French or Latin that were declared to be obligatory. It was claimed that Speransky, the upstart, was exploiting the tsar's favour by instigating revolutionary measures.

Most vociferous of his critics was Alexander's sister, the Grand Duchess Catherine Pavlovna, who had just married Prince George of Oldenburg. She complained bitterly to her brother that her husband's reports as Governor-General of Tver and other provinces should pass through the normal government departments, rather than be seen and dealt with exclusively by himself.

Added to Catherine's antagonism was that of General Arakcheev, the tsar's instructor in the arts of war at Gatchina, a man both autocratic and brutal. Now Minister of War, he believed Speransky to be dangerously left wing.

Conflict between the members of the hierarchy in the Russian government rose to a crescendo as the country faced the threat of war. Negotiations between the emperors of France and Russia continued but relations became increasingly strained. The tension rose as resentment mounted in Russia against the Continental System, which was ruining the country's trade. The climax came in December when Alexander learned that Napoleon, having annexed all the northern coasts of Germany, was proposing to take over Oldenburg. This direct contravention of the agreement arranged at Erfurt forced him into action. On 31 December he consented to the tariff decree, by which goods coming overland from Europe were heavily taxed, while restrictions were removed on those entering Russian ports. Trade with maritime countries, including Great Britain, the main outlet for Russian grain, hemp and flax, was thus established once more.

In St Petersburg it was now generally accepted that war with France was inevitable. The French Ambassador Caulaincourt, about to be recalled on health grounds, was told prophetically by the tsar:

> Should the Emperor Napoleon make war on me, it is possible, even probable, that we shall be defeated . . . I shall not be the first to draw my sword, but I shall be the last to sheath it . . . I should sooner retire to Kamchatka than yield provinces or put my signature to a treaty in my conquered capital which was no more than a truce.[34]

Fanned by the impending crisis, hostility towards Speransky increased. A sharp rise in taxation, to finance the expanding army, infuriated the landlords who felt themselves penalised by the expenditure of a man whose very loyalty had been questionable for some time. So great was the outcry of his enemies that Alexander, with much reluctance, complied with their request to allow the Chief of Police to watch Speransky. Nothing could be proved against him, but, faced as he was with an impending French invasion, Alexander's hands were tied. Convinced that even if Speransky was innocent, as he himself believed him to be, he knew that in continuing to uphold him he was placing not only his own life but also his vast empire in jeopardy. Accordingly, on the evening of 29 March, Alexander received Speransky in private audience in the Winter Palace. They talked for two hours. Then Speransky came out, obviously upset, and began pushing papers into a briefcase. Behind him the door then burst open again as Alexander, tears coursing down his cheeks, rushed to embrace him with fond farewells.

Speransky went home to find the Minister of Police waiting for him with a carriage in which he was carried off to exile in Novgorod, the great port on the River Volga.

As snow left the streets of St Petersburg in the spring of 1812, Russia faced a state of national emergency, greater than any known before.

On 20 April, in an audience with the Marquis de Lauriston, the new French ambassador, Alexander told him that while he was prepared to modify the Russian tariff to help French trade, he insisted that Napoleon should abide by his promise to evacuate Prussia. In addition he must remove his troops from Swedish Pomerania, and should Napoleon continue to advance his armies towards Russia he would consider it an act of war.

Meanwhile from St Petersburg regiments began marching for the frontier. On 21 April, Alexander himself left his capital to drive westwards to Vilna (now Vilnius), the third largest city in Russia at the time which, being only about ninety miles from Napoleon's newly formed Grand Duchy of Poland, lay directly before his expected advance.

Once there he was much entertained until, to return hospitality, he himself held a grand ball on the estate of General Bennigsen at Zakrêt on the outskirts of the city. There, while fountains played in the gardens beneath the light of a full moon and musicians of the Imperial Guard struck up the first notes of a mazurka, Alexander's Chief of Police, General Balashov, arrived to tell him that Napoleon, with an army numbering 600,000 men, was already across the Niemen, only sixty-five miles away. Russia had been invaded, without declaration of war.

CHAPTER FOURTEEN

Borodino

As Napoleon was known to be approaching Vilna, the tsar retired north-east to Drissa, a town on a tributary of the Dnieper some 160 miles west of Moscow. From there he made the long journey due east to Moscow where he appointed General Kutuzov, hero of the war with Turkey and now a man of sixty-seven, to the supreme command of his army.

At the same time Doctor James Wylie, still at the height of his strength at forty-four, became director of the medical department of the Ministry of War. The first indication of his efficiency as an administrator, soon to be so dramatically proved, is found in descriptions of the Russian army's withdrawal under darkness from Vitebsk at the end of July, when not a single sick man was left behind.[35] Furthermore General Langeron states in his memoirs that in the retreat of 1,200 versts from the Niemen to Moscow, during which the army fought two major battles, not even one sick or wounded soldier was left to be captured by the enemy.[36]

In early August, as Napoleon advanced across Russia, the first major battle took place at Smolensk. The town was left burning as the Russian forces retreated towards Moscow, leaving behind scorched fields to deprive the invaders of ripening crops. Hunger and fever were by now decimating the French forces but still they advanced with the force of a tempest destroying all in its path.

On 7 September 1812 the two armies fought at Borodino, a village about seventy miles west of Moscow, and near the town of Moskva. Napoleon's force of 130,000 men outnumbered the Russian troops, which were 120,000 strong. Kutuzov had ordered hastily built fortifications, mostly in the form of fleches, or trenches, built in the shape of arrows, on the idea of Prince Pyotr Bagration, who was in command of the Russian rearguard.

Doctor James Wylie was also prepared. Tents for field hospitals were in readiness, piled onto bullock carts, the drivers waiting for his instructions, relayed through orderlies, as to where they should be placed.

The battle began at six o'clock in the morning along a three-mile front. For six hours, until midday, the deadly thunder of cannons (the Russians had the advantage of 600 as opposed to the enemy's 500 guns) literally shook the ground. The French gained a slight advantage but, because Napoleon refused to send in the 20,000 men of his Imperial Guard, no decisive victory was gained.

Afterwards some of those involved in the battle remembered that it had been a beautiful day. An early-morning mist had cleared and the sun shone on the meadows on both sides of the River Kolocha. As the heat increased, the air became sweet with the scent of freshly mown hay.

Wylie, however, was not aware of it, as he and his team of surgeons began a battle of their own. Stretcher followed stretcher bearing men writhing in pain. Most had limbs or torsos shattered by cannon balls, grapeshot, or the deadly splinters of grenades. The work of amputation was exhausting for even the strongest of men. Survival of patients, operated on without anaesthetic, depended greatly on the speed with which it was performed. As the work went on the doctor's surgical aprons, however frequently changed, became saturated with blood. Canvas gave little relief from the sun so that, as the heat of the day increased, the stench within the tents became almost impossible to bear.

On the day of Borodino Wylie is known to have achieved the almost incredible feat of carrying out operations on at least 200 men. It is claimed that he made no distinction between friend and enemy, some of the wounded being French. Tolstoy pictured him in his novel *War and Peace*, calling him Villier, the Russian version of his name. As the mortally wounded Prince Andrey is carried to the dressing station, a doctor wearing a bloodstained apron, comes out of the tent, holding a cigar between the thumb and little finger of one of his bloodstained hands.[37]

Exhausted as he must have been, on the night after the battle, Wylie rode with General Platoff deep into the enemy lines. Only a man like Platoff, 'Hetman of the Cossacks of the Don', as Alexander named the commander of his legendary force, would have dared to have done what he did only hours after the guns had ceased to fire. But danger was an elixir to Platoff. Moreover, he knew that the mere sight of him and his men, swarthy, moustached and armed with deadly sabres, was enough stop any Frenchman from even trying to grab a rein.

Waiting until dusk was falling, with Wylie centred among them, the Cossacks rode into a field of carnage such as few of even the most hardened soldiers had ever before seen. On ground churned into mud, French soldiers, many of them wounded, their faces black with gun-smoke, thinking only of survival, were struggling to light camp fires. The guttering light showed what lay around them, dead and wounded men and horses, in a vision of hell.

The story, too grim to be forgotten even when many years had passed, was told by Wylie to his great-niece, who also affirmed that, while serving as a military surgeon throughout the Franco–Russian War, he had taken part in twenty battles and was wounded no fewer than three times. It is known that, on his own estimation, he had travelled with the army on foot or on horseback, in a carriage or on a sledge, more than 150,000 miles during the whole campaign.

The Russian losses at Borodino are claimed to have amounted to at least 44,000 men. Following the battle General Kutuzov, although not entirely defeated, resolved to adopt a strategy to conserve his remaining strength. At a conference in the village of Fili, knowing that the winter was coming and how severe it was likely to be, he laid down the policy that, as is now well known, would lure Napoleon to his doom. Under his leadership the fateful decision was reached that while with what remained of the army he would withdraw towards Moscow, he would not attempt to defend the city against Napoleon's overwhelming strength.

The strategy, so brilliant in conception, would nonetheless prove horrendous to achieve when it is remembered that within the city itself were thousands of wounded men. This must be called Wylie's greatest moment, for, as director of the medical department of the Ministry of War, he managed the near impossible feat of evacuating an estimated 30,000 casualties. His feat in doing so is all the more remarkable in view of the chaos that existed in the city as people tried to flee with their possessions through the crowded streets. Hundreds of horse-drawn vehicles, from carriages to the roughest farm carts, would have conveyed wounded men from the city to makeshift hospitals that had been erected beyond what was estimated to be the range of enemy guns.

Napoleon entered Moscow on 15 September to find the city on fire. Such was the destruction that, after only thirty-five days, with much sickness in his near-starving army, he gave the order to withdraw. His troops returned westward, following the way they had come, where the ravaged land and buildings gave neither food nor shelter to ill and exhausted men. From Smolensk they continued towards the frontiers of Poland and Prussia, struggling through snow as the winter set in with devastating, bone-biting cold.

The Grand Army of Napoleon, which had swept so triumphantly into Russia, returned across the wastelands of that huge country to be virtually destroyed by sickness and starvation induced by the appalling weather of those winter months.

CHAPTER FIFTEEN

The Agony of Failure

Wylie soon returned to St Petersburg as word reached him that the tsar himself was ill. He was suffering from erysipelas, a streptococcal infection which produces painful inflammation and a deep red colouring of the skin. The disease, which affected his leg, was thought to be aggravated by the mental stress and exhaustion induced by the news of Moscow's destruction, for which Alexander was thought to be much to blame.

The strength of anti-imperial feeling in St Petersburg became obvious when, on 27 September, the eleventh anniversary of his coronation fell due. As he drove through the streets with the Empress Elizabeth to attend a service of celebration in the Kazan Cathedral, there was ominous silence in the streets, the atmosphere tense with resentment. Yet these same people, who with sullen faces now lined the streets, were the ones who had so ecstatically welcomed their 'little father' on his return from the defeat of Austerlitz.

As the royal party entered the cathedral there was not a single cheer. 'I happened to glance at the tsar and, seeing the agony of spirit he was undergoing, I felt my knees begin to tremble beneath me' wrote a lady-in-waiting to the empress, remembering the humiliation that Alexander was forced to endure.

Two days later the official news reached St Petersburg that Moscow, burned and ruined, was now occupied by the French. The tsar, in a state of mental anguish, spent the next month almost entirely in the enchanting imperial villa on Kammionyi Island, lying at the mouth of the Neva in the Gulf of Finland.

Wylie, in constant attendance to the tsar, did all that was possible to help him as he wrestled with self-recrimination over the loss of life and honour to himself and his country and for the deaths of thousands of soldiers for which he was being held responsible by his subjects.

73

It did not help that while Alexander struggled with the demons in his mind, his sister Catherine chose that moment to harangue him, telling him in a letter that he was openly blamed. 'You broke faith with Moscow, which awaited your coming with desperate longing . . . but I leave you to judge the state of affairs in a country whose ruler is despised.'[38]

Alexander answered her carefully, pointing out that he had not gone back to Moscow because of the vital importance of a meeting with the Swedish Count Bernadotte, with whom he had made an alliance only six months before. Also, by his presence, he had not wanted to undermine the authority of General Kutuzov as his commander-in-chief.

'Perhaps I am even bound to lose friends on whom I have most counted,' he wrote sadly, but assured her that, in spite of all the vindictive words she had written, as he rightly guessed in a burst of uncontrollable temper, his undying love for her remained unchanged.

Around this time, as he struggled with depression, and inspired by his wife's Christian faith, he found comfort in the books of the Old Testament, particularly in the Psalms. 'I simply devoured the Bible,' was how he put it, 'finding that its words poured an unknown peace into my heart and quenched the thirst of my soul.'[39]

Peace offerings came from Napoleon, but Alexander, with all the stubbornness of his nature, refused even to countenance the idea of making any form of compromise 'with the modern Attila', which was how he had come to view the French emperor.

CHAPTER SIXTEEN

Victor of the North

On 18 October a detachment of the Russian army attacked and defeated the French, who were under the command of Marshal Murat, at Tarutino. The next day Napoleon left Moscow with the main body of his army.

Word then reached St Petersburg that General Kutuzov was driving back Marshal Murat's vanguard south-west of Moscow and soon it was known that the city itself was once more in Russian hands. Cannons fired and bells rang out in jubilation in St Petersburg as the tsar, along with all his family, the members of his government and the diplomatic corps, went to the Kazan Cathedral to give thanks for the deliverance of the former capital of the country from the invading foe.

This time, as the tsar left the cathedral, the watching onlookers spontaneously burst into shouts of applause. Their little father had been vindicated. He was their hero once more.

On 23 October Napoleon's advance guard, having crossed the River Luzha, entered the old town of Maloyaroslavets where, the next day, in a fierce battle, both sides lost an estimated 7,000 men.

Winter that year came early. The Neva froze over in the second week of November. Both Russian and French armies were by then struggling over roads made almost impassable by drifts of freezing snow. On 3 November the Russians defeated the French at Vyazma and on the 17th Marshal Ney left the town of Smolensk. On 5 December Napoleon himself left Russia to return to France, deserting all that remained of his army to retreat in what proved to be the cruellest period of a winter that killed more surely than bullets or cannon fire.

Roads, particularly in the more remote parts of the country, became so blocked with snow that the doctors and surgeons of the

Russian medical units, on the long front greatly undermanned, found it almost impossible to procure medicines. Also, as the Russian army advanced, the problem of finding adequate housing for temporary hospitals became increasingly acute.

On 13 December old General Kutuzov, exhausted by the weather and by the great responsibility of command, reached Vilna, the city now ruined by fighting with most of its finest buildings either destroyed or damaged by bombardment and fire. Kutuzov, in dispatches, complained that his army was exhausted. He wished to end – or at least call a truce to – the campaign. But Alexander would have none of it. He gave orders that fighting must continue until every Frenchman had left Russian soil. Excitement fuelling his energy, he determined to return to the front. Wylie of course would have to go with him. Nothing would hold him back.

And so, once more, they were off, both dressed in uniform as they raced in *droskys* (open four-wheeled light carriages) to the south-west. Leaving in darkness on 19 December, and constantly changing horses, they travelled over 400 miles in the space of only four days. Reaching Vilna just before dawn, Alexander laughingly proclaimed that the biting cold of the journey had cost him the end of his nose.

There, although welcomed with fireworks and much rejoicing, they soon found appalling conditions within the largely ruined town. The Russian army had been decimated by typhus fever, a disease endemic among men living at close quarters, being transmitted by fleas. Alexander is also known to have visited the French hospitals and Wylie, who on his own word accompanied him throughout the campaign, must also have witnessed horrors. In one vaulted building, by a flickering light, they saw corpses piled against the walls, living men still among them.[40]

Leaving Vilna on 9 January, Alexander, based at temporary headquarters at Meritz on the Niemen, ordered the army to cross the river into Prussia. Meanwhile he sent a secret message to Frederick William, suggesting a new alliance. Subsequently both Prussia and Sweden joined in the war against France. Meanwhile Napoleon's stepson, Eugène Beauharnais, left in command of the French army, retreated across the same ground over which Napoleon had advanced only five months before.

The tsar himself saw the deliverance of his country entirely as an act of Providence. 'Placing myself firmly in the hands of God I submit blindly to his will,'[41] he wrote to his friend Prince Golitsyn, a reformed libertine now pious as the tsar himself. Again and again he reread the eleventh chapter of the Book of Daniel, which prophesises how the invincible King of the South will be defeated by the King of the North.

The tsar's aides found it difficult to understand him. Wylie alone came closest to identifying the cause of his moods of elation and depression as being linked to the enormous weight of responsibility that, since the death of his father, he had been forced to bear.

In mid-March Alexander travelled still further west to meet Frederick William at Breslau. The Prussian king was now a widower, his lovely wife Louise, with whom Alexander had enjoyed such a happy flirtation, having died nearly three years before, in July 1810.

Two weeks later Frederick William returned to a joyous welcome in his own capital of Berlin. Following this, in the last week of April, and again with much celebration, Dresden was liberated from the French.

But by now resistance was strengthening. Napoleon had amassed a large number of conscripts to reinforce the army decimated during the long retreat. Kutuzov warned Alexander of the danger of an imminent counter-attack, but, on 10 April, the old general who had served him so loyally collapsed and died of a stroke. Alexander then appointed Wittgenstein, who had first routed the French near Moscow, to replace him, but many Russian senior staff resented this, on account both of his advancement over men older than he and his German birth.

Meanwhile, only two days after the general's death, on 2 May Napoleon mounted the attack that Kutuzov had foreseen, near the town of Lützen in Saxony, about forty miles south-west of Leipzig and eighty from Dresden. He was actually looking at the battlefield when the sound of cannon fire caught his ear. Immediately assessing the situation, he ordered Marshal Ney to act as a decoy by heading towards the town while he with his main army of about 110,000 men launched a massive assault on the allied army's flank. It might have been a total disaster on the scale of Austerlitz. But the French troops were exhausted and did not have the cavalry to pursue the combined force of Prussians and Russians, which, under Blücher and Wittgenstein, were forced to retire.

Both sides suffered terrible casualties in what was strategically a victory for the French. This time, unlike at Borodino, where the enemy had been entrenched on the battlefield, the wounded could not be carried to safety before the order came to cease fire. Wylie, as director of the medical services, could not under the circumstances be blamed for this.

On 10 May the Russian army re-crossed the Elbe. The King of Saxony submitted to Napoleon and the French again took Dresden, where Alexander and Frederick William had been welcomed so ecstatically only two weeks before.

Metternich, the Austrian foreign minister, was the first to initiate a peace. But it was Napoleon himself who sent Prince Caulaincourt, his former ambassador to St Petersburg and personal friend of the tsar, to arrange an armistice with Russian diplomats. The terms being at last agreed, a truce was signed on 2 June.

A fortnight later Alexander, who now knew of Wellington's victories in Spain, joined Metternich in Austria to discuss terms of what was hopefully envisaged as a lasting peace. At what became known as the Reichenbach Convention, it was decreed that Napoleon must agree to abandon not only all claims to the territories he had annexed belonging formerly to Prussia and Austria, but also to the dissolution of the Grand Duchy of Warsaw. Most importantly, should he fail to agree to these terms, Austria would join with the allies to fight against him until all of Europe was free.

Metternich went straight from Reichenbach to Dresden, where Napoleon reacted with predictable fury to the suggestions that were laid before him. He did, however, eventually agree to send a representative to a peace conference in Prague, but refused to give any firm commitment to meet the allies' demands. Emperor Francis, unwilling as he was to fight Napoleon, his son-in-law, conceded to Metternich's decision that only a combined advance against France itself could bring an end to the war. Napoleon continued to ignore suggestions of any form of compromise, and on 8 August the truce, after only two months, ended in a resumption of war.

CHAPTER SEVENTEEN

The Battle of the Nations

On 12 August 1813 the Austrians joined Russia, Britain, Prussia and Sweden in a new coalition against the French. On the 26th the combined armies stormed Dresden, headquarters of Napoleon, but were driven back with heavy losses. The next day Barclay de Tolly refused to order a counter-attack on ground that had become a quagmire due to pouring rain. Confusion resulted at headquarters, and Alexander missed death by inches as the French made a sudden and unexpected attack.

With Alexander was Lord Cathcart, the British ambassador to Russia, talking to General Moreau (another who, like Count Bernadotte, had deserted Napoleon to join the allies) when a cannon ball went straight through the body of Moreau's horse, breaking both of its rider's legs. General Wilson, who was also present, heard him cry out as his horse collapsed. '*C'est passé avec moi! Mon affaire est faite.*'

Alexander, seeing this happen, and oblivious to the efforts of his aides who begged him to retire to safety, immediately ordered that Moreau should be carried to the nearest village where he knew that Wylie was operating on soldiers already taken wounded from the field.

As the French general was brought to him on a stretcher, ashen-faced with shock and loss of blood, Wylie knew on the instant, as he saw bones protruding through skin, that there was only one thing he could possibly do to try to save his life. Death from infection or gangrene was inevitable should the shattered limbs remain. There was little chance that the general would survive the operation but, seeing no alternative, Wylie was forced to take action. Therefore without anaesthetic, and with soldiers holding the patient down, Wylie carried out a double amputation of Moreau's legs. Amazingly the general survived the operation but, despite Wylie's constant

79

attention, the slim chances of recovery, which to him had been so obvious at first sight, faded as, weakened by fever and delirium, he died after five days.

General Wilson, recording this incident, also praised the remarkable bravery of the Cossacks. He was there when a Cossack, struck by a cannon ball, arrived after a ride of twenty miles at Wylie's field hospital. Horrified, he watched as Wylie, again without anaesthetic, amputated the arm from the shoulder joint in the space of a mere four minutes. Afterwards the man spoke lucidly and next morning, having drunk some tea, he walked about the room before being driven home in a cart without springs for a distance of fourteen miles.

From what Wilson writes it is evident that Wylie, now in his early fifties, was much respected, not only in his own profession but throughout the army as well. Wilson himself, despite his seniority, came in for a tongue-lashing when an accident in a *drosky* resulted in deep cuts on his legs. Wylie ordered him to stay in bed but Wilson disobeyed him, hobbling about on duty the next day. Inevitably his legs and ankles swelled up, whereupon Wylie gave the general such a dressing-down that, as he himself confessed, he 'remained indoors and wrote despatches until he gave me permission to go out'.[42]

Wylie himself had now become prosperous to an extent that even a few years previously would have been beyond his wildest dreams. He who had earned 400 roubles as a regimental surgeon could also see now by his income how much he was appreciated. Apart from his salary, he received the village near Minsk that was named after him – Vileiskoye – as a life estate. Following the publication of *The Pharmacopoeia*, by supreme order, he had been awarded a lump-sum payment of 20,000 roubles which he had deposited with the St Petersburg Post Office. Confident now of his future, he also received the annual pension of 1,875 roubles for his participation in the Battle of Borodino.[43] The penniless young émigré from Kincardine was now a man of substance in the country that, increasingly, he regarded as his own.

The fate of Europe hung in the balance but in August 1813, Napoleon, brilliant strategist as he was, missed his chance. Immediately after his victory at Dresden, when he could have annihilated the allied army, he allowed it instead to retreat into Bohemia. On 29–30

Sir James Wylie Bt. wearing his many decorations.

Wylie's coat of arms, designed by Alexander I.

LEFT. Empress Elizabeth, wife of Alexander I.

RIGHT.
General Aleksyei Arakcheev.

Queen Louise, wife of King Frederick
William III of Prussia.

Maria Naryshkin, mistress of
Alexander I.

General Mikhail Kutuzov, commander
of the Russians during the Napoleonic
war.

Mikhail Speransky, secretary to
Alexander I.

ABOVE LEFT. The Grand
Duchess Catherine Pavlova,
favourite sister of Alexander I.

ABOVE RIGHT. The Dowager
Empress Maria Feodorovna.

RIGHT. Alexander I in 1818.

Equestrian portrait of Alexander I by Franz Kruger.

RIGHT. The only known portrait of Feodor Kuzmich

BELOW. Kuzmich's cell in Siberia

August the combined allied army defeated a smaller French force at Kulm in northern Bavaria. A French legend contends that General Dominique Vandamme, when taken prisoner, accused by Tsar Alexander of being a brigand and a plunderer, retorted that he was neither, but 'my contemporaries and history will not reproach me for having my hands soaked in the blood of my father'.

This cruel jibe, if true, did not seem to lessen Alexander's delight in the victory when he is said to have ridden from the field with jubilation shining on his face. Seeing a party of wounded soldiers being carried to a field hospital in a cart, he thanked them, asked how he could help them, and called them his comrades in arms.[44]

Subsequently, in the Battle of Leipzig, fought between 16 and 19 October, Alexander, by forcing the Austrian commander-in-chief Schwarzenberg to change the deployment, largely decided the issue. Known as the Battle of Nations, because of its size and the sheer numbers of troops that took part, an allied force of 400,000 with an estimated 400 cannons opposed a French army numbering only 200,000, with about half the number of guns.

On 16 October the Austrians attacked first from the south but were repulsed. Then the Prussian Marshal Blücher, approaching the city from the north, was held off by the French Marshal Marmont's strong defence. At this point Alexander insisted that the Russian reserves be immediately moved up. Two days later a massive combined force of the Swedish army under both Count Bernadotte (formerly one of Napoleon's marshals, but now, since 1810, after a stormy relationship with the emperor, heir to the Swedish throne) and General Bennigsen, totalling 350,00 men, moved like a deadly colossus against the city walls. The French fought gallantly but eventually were overcome by sheer weight of numbers and relentless murderous gunfire. Napoleon ordered a withdrawal through the city but the single bridge across the River Weisse Elster was prematurely mined. At least 20,000 men of the French army found themselves trapped. Many tried to swim to avoid being taken prisoner, the wounded Marshal Poniatowski being among those who drowned in the swift freezing water.

The conquest of Leipzig resulted in appalling casualties on both sides, 36,000 men being left either sick or wounded in the town. One resident wrote that 'the city had been transformed into one vast hospital, 56 edifices being devoted to that purpose alone.'[45] Wylie's team of surgeons was stretched to the limit, struggling to perform amputations in the requisitioned houses where lack of sanitation was one of the main reasons for the many recorded deaths.

Despite the dreadful loss of life, however, the battle of Leipzig was none the less a triumph for the allied force. Alexander, writing to his friend Prince Alexei Golitsyn on 21 October, told him:

'Almighty God has granted us a mighty victory over the renowned Napoleon after a four-day battle under the walls of Leipzig.'[46]

The French had now withdrawn from Germany. On 5 November the tsar reached Frankfurt, travelling in his coach with the horses being changed frequently in accordance with his usual frantic speed. He remained there, conferring with the Austrian Foreign Minister, Prince Clement von Metternich, while the main allied army crossed the Rhine.

The Russian army stayed beside the Rhine for a period of seven weeks. During that time it was brought up to strength largely through men from the hospitals becoming well enough to rejoin their regiments. James Wylie, as director of the medical services, must receive most of the credit for an amazing feat of organization. Buildings had been requisitioned for use as hospitals along a line of march stretching for nearly 1,500 miles. Even more amazing was the fact that even during the many spells of appalling weather endured along the way, supplies of food and medicines had in most cases been maintained to the point where survival in the hospitals had surpassed the expectations of most of the military command.

It is nonetheless fair to say that, whatever Wylie's achievement, the biggest factor in maintaining the supply lines was that of the intendant-general George Kankrin, a man as efficient as Wylie himself.

Kankrin had risen to power through ability rather than high birth. Coming from Hanau, in Hesse, he did have a university education, but then lived in great poverty until his writing on military administration was noticed by Barclay de Tolly. First appointed to a position in the army's victualling department, he had soon shown his aptitude for figures and administration to the point where the feeding and equipment of the army, in its long march across Europe, raised him high in the tsar's estimation. His reward was to be given the position of Minister of Finance, which he held for the next twenty-one years.[47]

Kankrin's co-operation with Wylie is further revealed by the knowledge that it was on his instigation that the magazine carts, used to bring up ammunition, were converted into the makeshift ambulances which conveyed the wounded from the battlefield, in which way many lives were saved.

On 1 February 1814, at La Rothière, the allies won their first victory on French soil. Alexander, impatient as ever, wanted to move towards Paris, but negotiations were prolonged by the arrival of the British Foreign Secretary, Viscount Castlereagh.

The war, however, was far from over. Napoleon, having retrieved thousands of troops from Spain, shortly defeated Blücher's army in battles lasting over five days.

On 21 March, as Napoleon confronted the whole of the combined army commanded by Schwartzenberg, he knew he had no option but to retreat. He then made what proved to be the fatal decision of abandoning the defence of his capital to attack the enemy's lines of communication on the Rhine.

At Vitry, on 24 March, Alexander, having summoned Frederick William and the leading generals to a council of war, insisted that the march towards Paris should begin on the following day.

The French attacked again at La Fère-Champenoise, where Alexander, hoping to avoid further casualties, sent an officer with a flag of truce in the hope that they would surrender. But the man was killed as he approached the lines. Alexander, still determined not to waste life unnecessarily, then put himself at the head of his chevalier guards and dashed into the compact mass of French troops, who scattered in every direction without a shot being fired. The French general in command, who surrendered his sword to Alexander in the square, was astonished to learn that it was the tsar himself who, at great personal risk, had led the cavalry charge to prevent a massacre.

The road to Paris was open. The next day, as the allied armies advanced, Alexander rode alongside his columns. 'My children,' he said to his guards, 'it is but a step further to Paris.' They responded: 'We will take it, father. We remember Moscow.'[48]

When in Moscow, Napoleon had so admired the city's golden cupolas that on his return to Paris he had gilded the dome of the Hôtel des Invalides (the hospital built by Louis XIV for old soldiers) and now as they neared the city they saw the gold glitter in the sun. On the morning of 31 March 1814, Alexander triumphantly entered the capital city of the man who had captured his own.

CHAPTER EIGHTEEN

Paris

The people of Paris went wild with excitement at the sight of the fabled Tsar of Russia. Crowds lined the streets to see Alexander, who had such a good seat for a horse, riding astride the dark bay mare which, in times of their friendship, had been a gift from Napoleon. In his dark green uniform, with golden epaulettes flashing in the sunshine, he epitomized the conquering hero, raising his arm in salute to the rim of the plumed hat crowning his fair, curling hair. Women screamed with delight as Alexander rode through the main streets of the city and into the Champs Élysées. Gasping with delight, they saw the Imperial Guards, cuirasses gleaming, riding horses as magnificent as themselves. Then some drew back in terror, clutching their children to their skirts at the sight of the moustached, swarthy-skinned men, as the murmured word 'Cossacks' drifted through the crowds. These were the legendary barbarians, famed for their ferocity and rapine. If the stories told of them were true, doors must be locked and windows barred. No one in Paris would be safe.

Beside the Marley Horses, sitting astride his own perfectly trained mare, Alexander took the salute of his columns of splendidly mounted cavalry and regiments of infantry until late in the afternoon.

He had meant to stay at the Elysée Palace but Nesselrode, the former commercial envoy to Paris who had now become his secretary, received a mysterious message that the palace had been mined by Napoleon's agents and therefore was highly dangerous to inhabit. This proved to be false information but Alexander nonetheless decided to accept Talleyrand's offer of part of his house, which stood most conveniently at the corner of the Rue St Florentin and the Rue de Rivoli.

Here the tsar, along with most of his entourage, occupied the whole of the first floor. Despite the number of rooms there was still not space for everyone. Wylie's great-niece wrote that he stayed in what she described as 'one of the best hotels'. Nonetheless the tsar kept his doctor close to him during those weeks of April 1814 when Alexander, briefly the most powerful man in Europe, held dominance over the discussions regarding the ruling of France.

In Talleyrand's house the tsar was protected night and day by guards of his own Semeonovski regiment. In the streets there was some disturbance as the citizens celebrated their freedom from a dictator's rule and the officers of the Tsar's Guard stopped the mob hauling down Napoleon's statue in the Place Vendôme. Vigilance was vital, for Napoleon was only a few miles away at Fontainebleau. Even more threatening was the news that Marshal Marmont, with a division of the French army stationed near Paris, was still defiant of surrender. The city remained in a state of tension as Caulaincourt, Napoleon's former ambassador to St Petersburg and one of his closest aides, hurried back and forth to the palace of Fontainebleau, carrying dispatches between the French emperor and the leaders of the allies, in whose hands now lay the fate of France.

Convinced at last by his advisers that there was no point in continuing the war, Napoleon sent envoys to Alexander with his offer to abdicate in favour of a regency for his three-year-old son. Accordingly, at three o'clock in the morning on 5 April, the tsar received Caulaincourt and the marshalls Ney, Marmont, and Mac-Donald in the first floor of the former foreign minister's house. Caulaincourt used all of his persuasive powers to convince Alexander to accept a Bonaparte regency, but Talleyrand, whom the tsar then consulted, told him on no account to allow this as a regency would undoubtedly be influenced by Napoleon if held in name by his son.

Alexander then confronted the envoys with his decision. Regency was unacceptable, he told them. Stability was a necessity for France. Napoleon must abdicate unconditionally. He would receive an adequate pension in whatever place of exile it was decided he should live. By now it was known that even as Marshal Marmont had joined the conference his corps, the last loyal contingent of Napoleon's once omnipotent army, had deserted him to join the allies.

Napoleon, on word of this, accepting at last that all was lost, put his name to the act of abdication on 6 April. Just a week later, on 13 April, the Treaty of Fontainebleau, signed first by the leaders of the four major powers, Russia, Prussia, Austria and Britain, was agreed. The document was then taken to Versailles by Caulaincourt, so that Napoleon could add his signature.

On receiving it, the French emperor, unable to accept the humiliation to which it was demanded he should put his name, attempted to end his own life with poison, but failed, perhaps deliberately. Once the treaty was ratified, Napoleon was granted both the sovereignty of Elba, and a pension of approximately 2,000,000 francs. He then left France for the island off the north-west coast of Italy, chosen as his place of exile by his one-time friend and ally, the Tsar of Russia himself.

CHAPTER NINETEEN

Celebration, Love and Sorrow

Paris was soon *en fête*. Nature itself seemed to welcome the conquerors. The warm sun shone from a clear sky, bringing chestnut trees bursting into flower. Gardens, scented with lilac, were bright with spring flowers and birds sang joyfully from dawn until the fall of night, heard even above the cacophony of hawkers shouting their wares and of horse-drawn vehicles in the streets.

While much involved in diplomacy, Alexander also enjoyed the city's social life. Balls were given in his honour. Fashionable ladies, whose husbands, sons and lovers, had so recently fought against him, competed to entertain him. He waltzed with the wives of generals and – susceptible as ever – fell in love again.

Extraordinary as it seemed, both then and ever after, the lady who inflamed his passion was none other than Josephine, she whom Napoleon had loved so passionately but had abandoned to marry the daughter of Emperor Francis of Austria in order to produce his longed-for heir. Exiled as he was in Elba, Napoleon himself must have marvelled at, and perhaps even rejoiced in, the irony of the man with whom he himself had enjoyed such a contrast in relationships, now being involved with the woman who would remain his enduring love.

Marie Josèphe Rose de Tascher de la Pagerie, as was Josephine's original name, had lived through much triumph and tragedy in her life. Born on a slave-worked plantation on the West Indian island of Martinique, she still spoke with a Creole accent, husky but attractive to the ear. She had first married Vicomte Alexandre Beauharnais, father of her son and daughter, Eugène and Hortense. Fêted by Paris society, both for her beauty and her charm, her world had dissolved in the revolution of 1793 when she and her husband had been imprisoned and he killed by the guillotine. Surviving and ever more ambitious, she had taken a series of influential lovers, until the young General Napoleon had been entranced by her at first sight.

Saddened as she was by her divorce from him after a marriage of thirteen years, she nonetheless retained some of the magic which had so enslaved him. Even at fifty, and now grown rather stout, she still possessed much of the beauty which had dazzled so many men's eyes. Nonetheless both time and hardship had taken their toll. Josephine, as Napoleon had called her and as she was now known to the world, was becoming physically frail and Alexander's relationship with her was to end as sadly as had that with Napoleon himself.

Time and again he called to see her at the beautiful house of Malmaison where she had lived since her divorce. On one occasion, when the King of Prussia had announced that he was bringing his two young sons to dine with her, she asked Alexander to come with his brothers Nicholas and Michael to help entertain them. Her daughter Hortense and her two little sons, Louis Napoleon and Napoleon Louis, were in the drawing room when the guests arrived. Alexander, who was fond of children, talked to the two boys, who told him that when they grew up they meant to become soldiers to fight the Prussians and the Cossacks! The King of Prussia, hearing this, was plainly not amused and their governess hastily took them away but on another occasion, the younger boy, later to be Napoleon III, slipped into Alexander's hand a gold ring which the tsar promised faithfully to keep for as long as he should live.

Excited by Alexander's attention, which made her forget her health, Josephine bought new dresses. One was a beautiful but flimsy creation, which she wore for a picnic near the Forest of Montmorency. The day was suddenly cold, as happens often in spring, and she caught a chest infection which turned into bronchitis. James Wylie, sent by Alexander to tend to her, strongly advised Josephine to rest. Nonetheless, embroiled as she was in refurnishing and re-decorating her house, she simply ignored her illness, refusing to stay in bed.

No amount of pleading from well-intentioned friends would stop Josephine, now once again the first lady of Paris, from holding a dinner and ball for Alexander, which would outdo any of the entertainments held in his honour by people who were, at least in her opinion, of lesser standing than herself.

Malmaison, for so long quiet and largely shuttered, was brought alive with running footsteps as servants scurried through the kitchens and the corridors of the floors above. Lights shone from every window, welcoming the guests. Reaching the entrance, footmen holding *flambeaux* handed them from their carriages to the open doors. French and Russian nobility who rubbed shoulders on the stairs included the Grand Duke Constantine, and Alexander's younger brothers, Nicholas and Michael, handsome in uniform, who had just arrived in France.

It is known that many of the tsar's entourage were present, therefore Wylie must have been among the press of people who saw Alexander take Josephine in his arms to lead off the dancing with a waltz. Later in the evening they slipped away together to walk through the garden to the hothouse where, much obsessed with gardening, she kept many rare and tender plants.

Emerging from the heated greenhouse, Josephine began to cough and shiver in the cold night air. She returned to the house exhausted. The adrenaline pumped into her system by the nervous energy that had sustained her throughout the hours of entertaining, suddenly drained from her body leaving her gasping for breath.

Her illness, now turned into full-blown pneumonia, grew worse over the next few days. Helpless doctors could do nothing but apply poultices and lower her temperature by bleeding, thus further weakening her already frail constitution. When told of what was happening to Josephine, Alexander turned in desperation to Wylie, begging him that as he had once saved Count Kutaisof, he could now do the same for Josephine by inserting a tube in her throat. But Wylie, knowing now that she was suffering from a malignant illness, was forced to tell him that in this case a tracheotomy would not only be useless, but would increase her suffering and destroy any chance of recovery she might still possess.

In Malmaison the servants moved quietly as Josephine struggled to stay alive. Five days after the ball that had taken such a toll of her strength, Alexander called again to see her. Hortense and her son Eugène were there, but Alexander, realizing when he saw her that she had only hours to live, left after a few minutes. Later that day the news that he now both dreaded and expected was brought to him. Josephine was dead.

Alexander was once more plunged into depression by the death of the woman he had all too briefly loved. Wylie did his best to reason with him but to small avail. Superstitious like most Russians, the tsar was now was becoming paranoid, convinced that he could only bring misfortune to anyone close to him.

Forced to face up to reality, he found himself dealing with the difficulty imposed by her funeral as it was discovered that the French army, still in the throes of changed allegiance, could not provide a fitting guard of honour to escort the coffin to the grave. Accordingly Alexander ordered that his own regiments, in full dress uniform, should stand to attention along the little country road from Malmaison to the church.

Thus by another stroke of irony was the great love of Napoleon Bonaparte, the man who had so nearly conquered Europe, escorted to her burial by the soldiers of the Tsar of Russia who, once his sworn ally, had led the forces of his enemies against him to defeat what he himself had believed to be the greatest army in the world.

There remained one more twist to the story of the strange and unnatural relationship between these two autocratic men who had held the fate of Europe in their hands. Alexander, having heard that the Elector of Hesse was trying to claim back the pictures in the Malmaison purchased from him by Napoleon for Josephine to enhance the beauty of her house, bought them himself from her heirs for a fair price that allowed them to pay off her debts. He took the pictures back to St Petersburg, where they were hung in the Hermitage as souvenirs of his victorious campaign.

Tourists were now once more pouring into Paris. Among them were some young Scotsmen, Archibald Alison and two young friends who came from the Forth valley. They brought letters of introduction to two men from their homeland, Lord Cathcart, the British ambassador to Russia, and Doctor James Wylie, physician to the tsar. Alison kept a diary in which he described the dignity, courteous manners and simple character of the tsar, to whom they were introduced.[49]

Wylie, having shown them around Paris, was entertained in return at a dinner party which they gave for sixteen Russians and Britons in the Restaurant Malpinot in Rue Saint Honoré, where, in an evening of great jollity, many toasts were drunk to both countries and to the heroes of the recent campaign.

In accordance with diplomatic agreement the Bourbon prince, who had been living in exile in England, returned to France as Louis XVIII. Born in 1755, he had succeeded his brother Louis XVI, whose son had died in the Temple Prison at the age of only ten. Louis XVI had in fact disowned his cousin, claiming that he had betrayed him out of personal ambition. So much did he hate him that, almost as he went to the guillotine, he gave the papers to his lawyer, banning him from the throne.

Following the revolution, Louis had wandered round Europe. For a time he had actually lived in Russia, at the invitation of Alexander's father, until Tsar Paul, in typical manner, had suddenly got tired of him, and he had found his way to England. There he had lived at Hartwell House in Buckinghamshire for fourteen years. Returning now to France, his brother's will was disregarded as he was proclaimed king.

A man of fifty-nine and a widower, Louis proved to be rude and arrogant. Long-nosed and heavy-featured, he used his considerable weight to push himself forward through doors in front of everyone else and, once at the dining-room table, insisted on being served first before any of his guests. Alexander remarked bitterly that anyone seeing his behaviour would think that he had come to return him to his throne, instead of it being the other way around. Nonetheless, despite his personal dislike of the man, he managed to stay outwardly civil and remain on equable terms.

The Peace of Paris, in which the tsar had played a major part as a negotiator, was signed on 31 May 1814. Once the details were completed, Alexander, who had now been absent from Russia for almost five months, began to plan his return.

However, an invitation from the prince regent to visit England made him change his mind. Accordingly, on 5 June, he reached Boulogne where HMS *Impregnable*, commanded by the regent's sailor brother, William, Duke of Clarence, waited to take him across the Channel to a country he had long wished to see.

CHAPTER TWENTY

England

Tsar Alexander travelled to England together with Frederick William of Prussia, Count Tolstoy and the fierce and intrepid hetman of the Cossacks, General Platoff. With him also went James Wylie, now once more gravely concerned for the tsar's physical and mental health. Deeply saddened by Josephine's sudden death, he was plunged into one of his periodic fits of depression, which, while exacerbated by the strain of the recent negotiations, was also due to his being very tired. To make matters worse the sea was rough and the ship battled against a contrary wind.

Alexander, in addition to sea-sickness, might have been running a temperature for an onlooker among the crowd that had gathered to witness his landing was greatly disappointed at the sight of this promised hero, who, she described as plump and very pink in the face.

Welcomed to Dover by the thunder of cannons, the tsar came thankfully ashore. Among notable people gathered to greet him was a Mr Fector who, on seeing the tsar's obvious indisposition, asked him to stay the night. Alexander accepted with gratitude and, ministered to by Wylie, was well enough the next morning to continue the journey to London, this time, thankfully, by coach.

Reaching Canterbury, the Tsar of Russia and the King of Prussia were welcomed by the prince regent.[50] The initial exchange of courtesies appears to have been brief. The prince, a corpulent figure compared to both his visitors, had already taken umbrage over Alexander's decision to join his sister Catherine in the Pulteney Hotel in London rather than accept his offer of a suite of rooms in St James's Palace. Nonetheless, protocol insisted that royal visitors from abroad must be entertained. Tersely the prince informed them of forthcoming banquets to be held in their honour before, as they parted company, more compliments were paid. Then, climbing back into their coaches, they were off again, rattling over the highway on their way to London.

They drove through the Kent countryside, so aptly named the garden of England, in the full glory of early June. Alexander, although entranced by the vision of hop fields and carefully tended crops within hedgerows in a country so unlike the vast spaces of his own, was nonetheless still exhausted and unwell.

At Blackheath he was met by his Russian ambassador, Count Lieven, who informed him that huge crowds were waiting to see him near London Bridge. Hearing this the tsar lost his nerve. Since his father's death the fear of assassination had always nagged at his mind, and suddenly terrified of meeting a horde of people at close quarters, he ordered the coachman to take another road.

After some consultation, a different route into London was devised through Camberwell and Clapham. Eventually, having crossed the Thames over the bridge at Battersea, the horses clattered into Knightsbridge and thence into Piccadilly where, in the Pulteney Hotel, his sister Catherine waited for him to arrive. Watching from a window she saw him, in his dark green uniform, climb out of the coach and, raising his eyes to her, gallantly blow her a kiss.

The Pulteney Hotel was then one of the smartest establishments of its kind in London. Thick carpets muffled the footsteps both of visitors and the ever attendant staff. Chairs and sofas were upholstered in plush and velvet, the wallpaper heavily embossed, and the chandeliers and brass fittings had been polished until they shone. Mr Escudier, the owner, resplendent in high winged collar and black frock coat, bowed from the waist, nearly overcome with honour as the Tsar of Russia entered his spacious hall. Behind him his wife trembled with excitement in her best bombazine gown, as she carried out the curtsey she had been practising for days. In turn, behind her, the senior members of the staff gave an equally obsequious greeting to the highly honoured guest.

Alexander, having acknowledged them, went leaping up the stairs into the arms of his favourite sister. Katya, as he called her, was now the widowed Duchess of Oldenburg, her husband Prince George having died of a fever at Tver the previous December. Catherine had left her two young sons to come to England, ostensibly to recover from depression caused by her husband's death, but more truthfully to enjoy herself away from the strictures of court mourning. Handsome rather than beautiful, small of stature and dark haired, she was still only twenty-four. Besides, as she herself said, she 'always looked her best in black'.

The choice to stay at the Pulteney appears to have been made by Catherine who, rather than staying in a palace, preferred the anonymity of a hotel. The reason for this, as she explained to her brother, was that she could not stand the advances of the Prince regent and his brother the Duke of Sussex, both known to be on the lookout for a bride. The prince regent was now divorced from Caroline, his excessively tiresome German wife, and the marriage of the Duke of Sussex to Lady Augusta Murray had been annulled because, contrary to the Royal Marriages Act, it had not been approved by the king.

According to Catherine, both princes looked her up and down as if she had been up for sale. The prince regent, for his part, declared that the Russian princess, who spoke English fluently, had had the temerity to tell him how to bring up his own daughter, with whom at that time he was on bad terms. Thus primed by their mutual animosity, the tone was set for disagreement even before Alexander arrived.

Brother and sister had much to talk about and soon they were joined by Count Lieven and his wife Dorothea, whose diary describes what then took place. Soon crowds gathered in Piccadilly, and people began shouting for the tsar. Alexander waved from the balcony but kept returning to the room to see if the prince regent, expected to make a courtesy call, had arrived. Shortly, however, a note came to say that the prince, who was then unpopular on account of his treatment of his wife, was afraid of being molested in the streets. Alexander then found himself left with no option but to make use of Lieven's carriage, in which he drove through the clamorous populace to meet the prince at his own residence of Carlton House.

The meeting was frigid. Prince George, never having been allowed to take part in military action himself, was intensely jealous of the tsar, now fêted throughout London as a hero.

But whatever the prince regent's attitude, the people of London made up for it, lining the streets and cheering wherever he and Catherine went. At the theatre people who did not have seats and boxes hired spaces in the foyer to see at first hand the handsome tsar and his dark-haired, striking sister, who wore a feather in her hat to give her height.

Alexander may have offended the prince regent but the people of London loved him as their own. Everywhere he went he was mobbed. Women, in particular, went into raptures, throwing posies at his feet. Now, even more than in Paris, he displayed the common touch. He shook hands and talked to those about him in the friendliest of ways. At Portsmouth, where he reviewed the fleet, he charmed not only the officers but also the sailors with whom, on a visit to one of the ships, he shared a meal. On another he drank some grog, issued to the crew each day at noon. 'You call it grog,' he said in his guttural English accent, 'I think it is very good.' And with that he poured out some for his sister who, as usual, was by his side.

The Russian tsar soon attracted the type of adulation these days given to stars of the media. So desperate were people to see him that in the mornings people got up early to watch him walking in the park with Catherine, or riding through what were then the fields of Marylebone to the villages of Hampstead and Highgate on the rising ground beyond. Crowds of excited citizens gathered round Westminster Abbey and the British Museum to watch them come and go. Hands were stretched out in the desperate hope that their idol would stop to shake them as he passed.

On more formal occasions the citizens of London saw Alexander, resplendent in gold and scarlet dress uniform, driving with his black-garbed sister to the banquets given by the City of London and the Prince Regent. A special journey was made to Oxford, where the university honoured both Alexander and Frederick William as the 'liberators of Europe'. Again there was a civil banquet before, on the next morning, the whole party – which included the prince regent, the Austrian Prince Metternich and the Prussian Marshal Blücher, together with a host of generals and diplomats – processed from Christ Church to the Sheldonian Theatre, where Alexander was made a Doctor of Civil Law.[51]

This was followed by a visit to the Duke of Marlborough at

Blenheim Palace, where the magnificence of Vanburgh's greatest creation was compared with the palaces designed by Francesco Bartolomeo Rastrelli in St Petersburg, so far away.

Returning to London, 'a dinner as sumptuous as expense or skill could make' was given for the visiting royalties by the City of London at the Guildhall. Wylie is known to have been present and must have witnessed the frigidity of the prince regent, who, annoyed by the tsar being late, partly because he had stopped to talk to Whig parliamentarians on the way, treated him and his sister to 'a haughty silence' throughout.[52]

Alexander's popularity with the people of London was as salt in a wound to the prince regent, who himself had been booed in the theatre with shouts of 'where's your wife?' at the height of the scandal over his divorce. To make matters worse Alexander soon became infatuated with the Countess of Jersey, a former mistress of the prince, which irritated him irrationally despite the fact that he had long since cast her off.

For Alexander himself it was a case of a new love replacing the old. The sorrow over Josephine's death at least partly vanished as, once again in pursuit of a pretty woman, he found a new zest for life. To James Wylie, long familiar with Alexander's mood swings, it came as a great relief to see him out of his depression and back in his normally ebullient frame of mind. So enamoured was he of the countess that he insisted on travelling back from Blenheim with great speed to attend a ball she was giving, at which he made up for his late arrival by dancing Scottish reels, which no doubt Wylie had taught him, until six o'clock in the morning.

Despite their private incompatibility, protocol demanded that the prince regent and Alexander must appear outwardly as friends. Together with Frederick William of Prussia, they rode in Hyde Park. On one occasion, as Princess Charlotte, the prince's daughter, appeared in her carriage, Alexander rode up to doff his hat and pay his respects to the pretty bonneted young lady, which were most joyfully received.

On another occasion, at Ascot Races, the tsar asked the prince as a special favour to knight his doctor, James Wylie, in honour of his achievements during the recent campaign. The prince agreed with good humour, borrowing General Platoff's sword to tap him on the shoulder as he knelt before him on the grass.

Later, during the same visit, and at Alexander's special request, Wylie was created a baronet of Great Britain by the prince. Alexander himself then sat down and drew out the design for the coat of arms which today can be seen engraved on a plaque on the rock on which his statue is mounted in St Petersburg. Consisting of a shield divided horizontally into two parts, the upper bears the imperial coat of arms of Russia above a silver sword. The lower portion contains a blood-stained glove, two five-pointed stars and a running fox. The shield is surmounted by an open helmet and a Cossack of the Don, mounted and charging at full speed. It is supported by two soldiers of the Zimeroff Guards, fully armed in ceremonial dress, and the Latin motto below reads: *Labore et Scientia* ('Labour and Science').

It would seem to have been at this time that the tsar presented his doctor with the large gold ring-seal. The seal was a carved red cornelian representing two Napoleonic soldiers. A Latin inscription on the gold circumference read 'To Jacobus Wylie from the Tsar of Russia *per cum felici*'. Sadly this ring was lost by a descendant, but a pair of pistols, believed to have been taken from Napoleon's carriage, were later given by Wylie to the Wellcome Museum.

The tsar had intended to travel on to Scotland and to sail back to Russia from Leith. This would have fitted in well with Wylie's plans, allowing him to visit Kincardine, where many of his family still lived. Janet is known to have made the long journey to St Petersburg, departing back to Scotland with several much treasured shawls.

His eldest brother William, however, now Master of the Public English School in Dundee, came down to London with his family to visit their now famous relation. The sight of the esteemed doctor, a tall, imposing man in his late forties, with decorations of foreign countries emblazoned on his uniform, both impressed and intimidated his relations. Long gone and near forgotten was the thin, rebellious young man who had sailed away to Russia at the age of only twenty-two. So long in fact had he been absent that they probably found it hard to comprehend some of his words, the Scottish accent of his youth being imbued with inflection of the Russian tongue. Lodged as he would seem to have been with the rest of the tsar's entourage in the Pulteney Hotel, he may even have found it difficult to get used to the food and customs of a country that now seemed foreign to him.

Reunited with his relations, he is known to have given valuable presents, in addition to a hundred pounds, to each of his five nieces. More importantly, he tried to persuade his nephew, the Reverend Doctor John Wylie, respected Church of Scotland minister at Carluke, to return with him to Russia as his secretary. But the young man refused, probably for family reasons, or else intimidated both by his uncle and the thought of going so far from home. Wylie bore him no grudge; years later, when his nephew did finally go to visit him in Russia, he was to receive yet more expensive gifts.

Also included in the present-giving was Madame Escudier, wife of the proprietor of the Pulteney Hotel, to whom Alexander presented a valuable brooch on his departure from the hotel. The tsar and his entourage left London on 22 June. Travelling to Portsmouth, both he and his sister were entertained by the prince regent, for the last time, on the royal yacht. At Spithead they saw the strength of Britain's navy as they watched a review of the fleet. Then moving on to Petworth, they said farewell to the prince regent before sailing to Ostend on 27 June.

CHAPTER TWENTY-ONE

'The First Medical Person in the Russian Empire'

Tsar Alexander, with his personal doctor and Surgeon in Ordinary, now Sir James Wylie, returned to St Petersburg on 24 July 1814. That Wylie had committed himself to his adopted country is proved by the fact that his engagement to an English woman, who lived in St Petersburg, although sanctioned by Alexander, was nonetheless broken off because she wanted to go back to England. Nothing would make him resign his high position in the country he now considered his own. If not a misogynist, he seems to have preferred the company of men to the point where a group of Russian military surgeons became his 'family' in whose undemanding company he liked to spend his time.[53]

While in England, the tsar and his doctor had visited hospitals in London where Wylie, thanks to his reputation, had found himself warmly received. The main hospitals were the Westminster, with ninety-eight beds, the London Hospital on the south side of White-chapel Road, and St Thomas's in Southwark, which had been much endowed by the wealthy merchant Sir Thomas Guy, founder of the infirmary on the opposite side of the road which to this day bears his name.

Also in London was Bethlem Hospital at Moorfields, the lunatic asylum famously featured in many of Hogarth's cartoons. Commonly known as Bedlam, it was a great tourist attraction, the visitors being allowed to peer at the antics of the 'unfortunates' as they were then termed. They were even permitted to bring long sticks with which to poke at them through the bars to enrage them into performing the antics thought amusing by their tormentors, to whom madness was a form of sport.

In the absence of records of their visit it seems unlikely that the tsar and Wylie were among the 96,000 visitors to the Bethlem Hospital that year. It is known, however, that they did visit several of the hospitals named above. Touring the wards they had found that, contagion now being recognized as a cause of disease, the beds were placed further apart. This was just one example of the advancement of medical science, thanks to the chance for experiment offered by the carnage of the recent war.

The war had also produced a more humane outlook towards the suffering of the men, who had hitherto been regarded as being as dispensable as the bullets they fired. Wellington, who had so caustically referred to his soldiers as 'the scum of the earth', had added that he would 'never fight a battle without them'.

Ironically, however, it was the French who had led the way in reforming conditions for the fighting men. Foremost among them was Baron Larrey, Napoleon's Surgeon General, who had invented the well-sprung ambulances, the *ambulances volantes*, by which wounded men were spared the agony of jolting carts. He had also perfected the art of surgery, famously amputating limbs in two minutes as his opposite number in Wellington's Peninsular army, Doctor James McGrigor, could vouch for, having witnessed him operating in Paris following the armistice with France. McGrigor, who kept a journal throughout the Peninsular War, describes how he, like Wylie, influenced his commander-in-chief – in his case the cantankerous Iron Duke – to establish the field hospitals which saved so many men's lives.

Unfortunately his diary ended with the armistice and, as we know, Wylie's own memoirs were destroyed. Nonetheless it is more than likely that the two men, both Scotsmen, and with so much experience to share, should have met, either in Paris or in London, to which, at the time of Wylie's visit, McGrigor had just returned. Appointed Chief of the Army Medical College (later the RAMC) at Millbank, he then held a position in British army circles similar to that of Wylie in Russia.

Wylie's importance in Russia is emphasized by a contemporary physician, Doctor Lyall, who, possibly jealous of his predominance in Russian medical circles, and of his influence with the tsar, described him as:

> One of the most notorious and powerful individuals in Russia . . .
> with not very brilliant medical talent, with very moderate
> scientific acquirements, and with much singularity and little
> refinement of manners. Sir James Wylie has risen from the most
> obscure parentage to be the first medical person in the Russian
> Empire.[54]

Wylie was obviously outspoken, a characteristic inherited from his
mother, but Lyall's envy shines through when he criticizes his work.

Prior to the reign of Alexander the care of the sick in the peasant
population had been left almost entirely to parish priests. Likewise
even the prestigious Guards regiments had only a few surgeons to deal
with the accidents and diseases inevitable among hundreds of men.
The Russian soldier was considered expendable, but it seems as
though it must have been Wylie who opened the eyes of the emperor
to the suffering and waste of life that was draining his army's strength.
Certain it is that, deeply concerned over the great losses among his
soldiers in the Crimea, the tsar asked him to produce a treatise on
considering 'preventive and curative instructions for the Russian
troops', and that subsequently, with typical efficiency, came the
medical papers on yellow fever and plague, written in his neat, small
hand in both Russian and French.

Already Wylie's *Handbook of Operations*, again much sneered at by
Lyall, had now been in print for nearly ten years, and reprinted
several times. Likewise his magnum opus, *The Pharmacopoeia Castrensis
Ruthiena*, again many times reprinted, remained the authorized text-
book on the subject for over half a century. Of still more lasting
importance are the scientific *Journal of the Royal Medico-Chirurgical
Academy* and *The Military Medical Journal*, established initially by Wylie
and which continue to the present day.

Amazing as it now may seem, during the first quarter of the
nineteenth century the three chief public offices in Russia were held
by men with Edinburgh degrees. While Wylie headed the medical
branch of the army department, James Leighton held a similar
position for the Navy and Alexander Crichton for the civil department. All three found themselves struggling against corruption,
endemic in all government offices throughout the land.

Lyall's obviously jaundiced view of Wylie may have sprung from the fact that, before being able to practise in Russia, Lyall was forced to pass the examination of the Medico-Chirurgical Academy as dictated by law. Although advised to bribe the professors he refused to do so and, to his own and everyone else's surprise, he passed successfully nonetheless.

Sir Alexander Crichton, on the other hand, was already distinguished as an expert on mental disorders before going to Russia as physician to Alexander I in 1804. On becoming head of the civil medical department he found his office to be infested with corruption which he struggled to remove. Most notably he wrestled with a bad outbreak of cholera in 1809 which, thanks largely to his competence, was eventually subdued. He also succeeded in organizing universal vaccination against smallpox, one of the most dreaded diseases of the time. Crichton, reportedly a very likeable man, was one of the many emigrants in Russia who made his fortune within a few years. Popular at court, he collected pictures, some of which remain in the Hermitage to this day.

Sir James Leighton, head of the medical department of the navy, was another of Wylie's compatriots against whom Robert Lyall vented his spleen. Lyall claimed in his autobiography that 'although the medical services of the Navy needed reorganizing, Doctor Leighton probably thought it better to take the salary and let the Russians get on with things themselves'.[55]

Despite Lyall's scathing assertion, Leighton's reputation is vindicated by a fellow physician, Doctor Robert Lee who, himself working in Russia at a later date, was taken round the Marine Hospital in St Petersburg. Noting in his own journal that 'Leighton had taken great trouble to set up an excellent surgical theatre and that the whole hospital was in very good order,' he added that he had found Leighton's medical views to be 'quite up to those of the most scientific doctors in London'.

Lee, having shortly left England, should at that point have known what he was talking about. Observant and literate, he left in his journal a vivid picture of life in Russia at that time. It is largely thanks to him that a clear picture emerges of the illness which was to affect Alexander in the final months of his life. A fellow Scot, Lee had much in common with Wylie, whom he held in great respect although, with twenty-four years between them, he was young enough to have been Wylie's son. Wylie had already been in Russia for three years when Lee was born in the Scottish Border town of Galashiels in 1793. Following in the footsteps of the man who was to become his mentor, he had taken his degree in medicine at Edinburgh University, aged only nineteen, in 1814.

While there, because it was a common topic, even if he did not buy a newssheet, he must have heard of the tsar's visit to London, widely reported as it was. The identity of the doctor who travelled with him, tall and distinguished as the emperor himself, probably escaped his notice for, unlike in Russia, Wylie's name in Scotland was known only to a few. Little could Lee, at that time just emerging on his career, have guessed at his own future involvement with the Tsar of Russia and with the man of his own profession who would fight such a desperate battle to save his life.

CHAPTER TWENTY-TWO

The Prophetess

On returning from England, Tsar Alexander remained in St Petersburg for only two months. Then he was off again, this time with his wife, the Empress Elizabeth, their horses as usual driven at a frantic speed, over the many miles to Austria, the most central empire in Europe, chosen as the venue for the great debate that would become known as the Congress of Vienna, aimed at settling the future of the continent.

On 25 September, together with Frederick William, King of Prussia, the tsar made a ceremonial entry into the Austrian capital. The Emperor Francis, having made over a whole wing of his Hofburg Palace to the Russian delegation, then spent the modern equivalent of £5,000,000 in entertaining his guests.

Alexander and Elizabeth borrowed Count Razumovsky's enormous Neoclassical palace to hold a banquet for a great number of guests – from 400 to 700 according to various writers of the time. The count's protégé Beethoven, although invited, was one of the few who did not attend, perhaps due to his deafness. The scene was remembered as magnificent. Fifty tables within the enormous panelled hall were set with porcelain and silver brought from Russia, as were the cucumbers, lettuces and cherries which came from the hothouses of the tsar's summer palace of Tsarskoe Selo. The room glowed with the light of thousands of candles, burning in the vast chandeliers. Guests were dazzled by the sheer ostentation of the spectacle but the sight that drew most eyes was that of the Russian empress, a slight, almost fairy-like figure, in a dress of shimmering silk and gauze enhanced with tiny pink roses. Declared by those who were present to be unsurpassable both for her beauty and graciousness, it was also to be remembered afterwards how, whenever they fell on his wife, Alexander's eyes shone with pride.

Later some chroniclers were to accuse the tsar of spending too much time in gaiety but, although he enjoyed the many entertainments, he came to the Conference of Vienna with a clear purpose in mind. Foremost among the problems which faced the assembled delegates were the position of Poland and the fate of Saxony. Alexander intended to restore Poland as a kingdom and to cede Saxony to Prussia, but both Britain, as represented by Castlereagh, and the Austrian Foreign Minister Metternich, spoke forcefully against this plan. A secret agreement signed by both men, together with the French Foreign Minister Talleyrand, who had cunningly exploited the jealousy between the delegates, resulted in Castlereagh's announcement that George III's government, under Lord Liverpool, would not agree to any reconstruction of Poland except that it be independent of Russia.

Alexander, frustrated, quarrelled openly with Metternich more than once, but at last a compromise was reached. Three quarters of Poland, known as the Duchy of Warsaw, became a subject kingdom of Russia, the remainder would be part of Austria. Saxony was to remain independent under King Frederick Augustus, although one third of his territory was to be ceded to Prussia. France, while forced back to her 1792 frontiers, was to be allowed to keep her former colonies.

In the middle of December, as was typical of him, Alexander, who had so much enjoyed the social life of Vienna, had a sudden change of mood. His health was partly to blame. The erysipelas broke out on his leg again, and Wylie made him sit with his leg in a bucket, filled with a block of ice, sent on the orders of the Emperor Francis every day. Also it was rumoured that he had syphilis, which, although feasible, cannot be proved.

It was at this point, his mental and physical health plainly at a low ebb, that he began an association with the mysterious Baroness Julie von Krüdner, who claimed to have visionary sight. Firstly, while still in Vienna he received a message from her telling him that he was 'one upon whom the world has conferred much greater power than the world recognizes'.[56] Then when she sent a warning of 'a storm approaching . . . the Bourbon lilies of France have appeared only to disappear' shortly before the news came of Napoleon's escape from Elba, Alexander became convinced of the woman's magical power. When Napoleon sent Alexander a copy of the secret treaty made between Austria, Great Britain and France, Alexander, having read the document, summoned Metternich to his side and told him that '*notre sainte loi commande de pardoner les offenses*'.

Alexander finally left the Austrian capital on 25 May. Reaching the town of Heilbronn on 4 June,[57] he had retired to read his Bible when his aide-de-camp, Prince Peter Volkonsky, tapped timidly on his door. A strange woman had arrived, he said, looking rather like a peasant dressed in simple clothes, but she claimed she was the Baroness von Krüdner and insisted she must see the tsar.

This was the first of many meetings. She spoke to him with words of hope and consolation, in his words, 'as though able to read my very soul'. We can only imagine what Wylie thought of her, suspicious of her integrity as he, along with so many others, must certainly have been. But he may have believed her harmless, perhaps even beneficial, as she seemed to bring comfort and tranquillity to Alexander's troubled mind.

From Heilbronn Alexander moved to Heidelberg, where he heard of the British and Prussian victory over Napoleon at Waterloo. He then travelled on to Paris, which he reached on 10 July. This time, rather than accepting the offer of Talleyrand's mansion, he stayed in the Elysée Palace, still associated in the minds of Parisians, as in Alexander's, with the Empress Josephine, whose town residence it once had been.

The trial of Napoleon's adherents was now the main talk of the city. Several of these desperate men, headed by General Lebedoyère, planned to overpower the guards at the houses where the allied sovereigns were staying and assassinate them all. The plan failed. Lebedoyère confessed and his wife threw herself at the feet of King Louis and then at those of Alexander, pleading that his life be spared. Alexander replied that, although he truly pitied her, he could not interfere with the decision of the French tribunals and Lebedoyère, accordingly, was executed.

Alexander knew that his life was in danger. On 7 August, at a ball held by the Duke of Wellington, a letter was handed to him signed 'the Captain of the Regicides' who threatened to kill him if he did not proclaim Napoleon's son as king of France. It is claimed that a bottle of poisoned wine was placed on his table and that his cook, who tasted it, nearly died as a result.[58]

The baroness pursued Alexander to Paris where he spent some time with her nearly every day. It was noticed that he became increasingly withdrawn, taking part in only formal ceremonies such as taking the salute of his own troops and standing beside Wellington, whom he greatly admired as, in the Place Louis XV, the Guards and the Highland regiments marched by in a review.[59] In September, at another ceremony, when Wellington and Marshal Blücher and the monarchs of Austria and Prussia were present, Julie von Krüdner actually stood by Alexander, wearing a straw hat.

Julie von Krüdner is thought to have been the inspiration behind the Holy Alliance, which, modified by Metternich, was signed by Alexander, Frederick William of Prussia and the Emperor Francis of Austria, on 26 September 1815.

This strange pledge was designed to unite the rulers of the continent by taking as their only guide 'the precepts of the Christian religion'. Emperor Francis, having read it, decided that it simply confirmed his suspicion that Alexander was mad. Nonetheless he signed it, although Metternich shared his doubts as to the sanity of the tsar. So too did Wellington, who happened to be with Castlereagh when Alexander came to explain his idea, and found it hard to keep a straight face.

Julie von Krüdner herself claimed the idea of the Holy Alliance as her own. However, by the time that the treaty, toned down by Metternich, was signed, Alexander, for some unexplained reason, had grown tired of her. Her association with him, however, had now become so well known that shortly after leaving Paris for the German states, suspected by the authorities of being a Russian spy, she was chased from town to town.

A decree of the Second Treaty of Paris declared Alexander King of Poland. Entering Warsaw on 7 November, wearing the Polish uniform with the order of the White Eagle, which he had re-established, he was loudly and joyfully acclaimed. He refused to accept the keys offered by civic dignitaries, saying he had come not as a conqueror but as a friend. Instead he partook of the traditional municipal gift of bread and salt.

'The Poles exhausted demonstrations of respect, joy, and attachment,' wrote Count Joseph de Maistre, the lawyer, diplomat and philosopher who, a native of Savoy, was the ambassador of the King of Sardinia to Russia from 1803–17.

The winter had now set in with heavy falls of snow so that it was not until 12 December that, after an atrocious journey over ice-bound roads, the tsar reached St Petersburg at last.

Once there he was back in harness, immediately shouldering the affairs of state. De Maistre, describing the tsar's amazing physical and mental resilience, describes how 'Yesterday he went to bed at three a.m., rose at six, and visited all the military hospitals. So active a mind would be useless if it did not command an iron body.'

The ambassador does not mention the even more surprising endurance of the tall, uniformed figure of Wylie, who despite the fact that he was nearly fifty, as head of the medical department was, as his great-niece testifies, dragged out of bed to be present beside the emperor on these exhaustingly thorough tours of inspection, which kept the hospitals and other civic authorities so constantly on the alert.

CHAPTER TWENTY-THREE

Rebuilding From the Ruins of the War

Alexander returned to St Petersburg to find the Persian ambassador waiting to see him. He brought with him presents from the shah sent with the intention of persuading him to restore the two provinces ceded by Persia to Russia in 1813. The gifts consisted of three elephants in black accoutrements and red leather boots to protect their feet from the snow. Sadly, however, the huge animals slipped about on the ice.

Alexander did not agree to the shah's request, to the great consternation of the Persian ambassador, who claimed he would lose his head as the result. He did, however, send his own envoy, General Yermolov , with presents of enormous mirrors, rich furs and crystal ornaments, which so pleased the shah that he agreed to forgo his demands.

The tsar left St Petersburg for Moscow in August. Then it was Warsaw in October, where he found great changes taking place. New houses were appearing and the streets of the city were paved. He then raced north to Vilna before returning to St Petersburg within a matter of days.

This was a time of innovation, as a new steam boat, one of the first in Europe, plied its way back and forth to Cronstadt (Kronstadt), Russia's great naval base. In the following year Alexander reviewed the fleet there before proceeding to Moscow where, with the rest of his family, he spent the winter. Here again, while staying in the Kremlin, in the very part used by Napoleon from where he had watched the city burn, he was constantly occupied at most hours of the day and night.

An Englishman visiting Moscow a short time later was amazed by the cleanliness and order in the hospitals and public buildings which were 'enforced by the constant, unexpected visits Alexander pays to them, for he is liable to appear and go through a minute inspection at any hour of the day, and sometimes in the middle of the night'.

Alexander had returned to Russia to find that the Medical Academy in Moscow, established by his grandmother, Catherine the Great, had been burned to the ground by the French. Ordering Wylie to replace it, he gave him a free hand.

Wylie had long since decided that the policy of importing doctors – many of whom were Scottish – into Russia, as established by Catherine the Great, was now greatly out of date. He believed it to be better by far to train native doctors, familiar with Russian customs and with indigenous disease.

Told that a house of three storeys with Doric pillars was available, he successfully approached the government for a grant of money to allow the building to be bought. Once converted, and with large extensions added, it became the centre for the new training college for doctors. The pediment, showing the cipher of Alexander I, bore the inscription in Russian: 'The Medical-Chirurgical Academy'.

A similar institution was commissioned in St Petersburg. As in Moscow, it was modelled on the Medical Society of Edinburgh University where Wylie had studied as a young man. Each Academy contained an anatomical museum and a botanical garden where much rhubarb, then thought a panacea for most illnesses, was grown. In addition there was a Medical Section, a Veterinary Section and a Pharmaceutical Section. Three languages – Latin, Greek and German – were compulsory, being essential to medical students, the first two for medical classification, and the third as the language in which many treatises were transcribed. The annual cost of the maintenance of the St Petersburg Academy alone was 169,000,300 roubles[60] while the building in Moscow took 147,000,340 roubles. In addition a sum of 69,000,650 roubles, common to them both, included pensions to professors, prizes to the students, uniforms for the pupils on taking up professions, and finally travelling expenses and the upkeep of libraries and museums.

Wylie remained head of both colleges for thirty years. In April 1836, a contributor to the *British and Foreign Medical Journal* paid tribute to his achievement with these words:

It is to Sir James Wylie that Russia is indebted for the organization of her medical schools both civil and military and it has been by his persevering industry that the medical academy of Petersburg and Moscow has arrived at the honourable rank which it now holds amongst medical institutions.[61]

Wylie, with the tsar's encouragement, had already begun transforming the military hospitals, which, at the time of his arrival in Russia, were in the most deplorable state. Old dilapidated buildings, dark and badly ventilated, infested with rats and other vermin such as lice, were, to the patients who entered them, practically a death sentence. Yet despite this he met with great obstruction in his attempts to modernize and reform these long-established institutions. The old Russian doctors, hidebound in their methods, were utterly opposed to change. To convince them, he hit on the simple but clever idea of placing plants in various windows. Those facing south sprouted happily while the others withered and died.

The new hospitals were built on the lines of the institutions which Wylie, with the tsar, enthusiastic as himself for improvement, had inspected in London and Paris. A doctor who visited the Military Hospital in Moscow in 1819, described it as situated in a high and airy suburb, with an elegant frontage and two extensive wings.

It contained twelve-hundred patients but is capable of receiving fifteen-hundred. Opposite the foreign burying ground are a number of one-storey, wooden, yellow painted houses, which belong also to this hospital and which are provided with beds for three-hundred-and-fifty sick. At this establishment everything seems conveniently arranged. There is a receiving room where the patients are examined by a physician or surgeon and accepted; a bathroom and baths well supplied with cold and warm water in which those admitted, when their state allows it, are all well bathed and cleaned, or in which the sick receive particular baths by order of the physician, and a room for the deposition of the patient's own clothes when they receive the dress of the hospital. Upstairs, in the centre of the front, a grand saloon with a lofty arched roof, embellished in the ends by

Corinthian pillars, contains pictures of Peter the Great, Catherine I, Elizabeth and Catherine II. From this hall is the entry into
the balcony opposite the summer gardens from which the view is
extensive and pleasant. This hall is designed for the reception of
the Emperor who never fails to visit this hospital when he comes
to Moscow.

Most of the wards are immensely large and capable of
containing a hundred-and-twenty beds. A single ward occupies
the whole breadth of the building, in the centre, running
lengthwise. Ranges of beds are disposed along the walls of
these wards. The bedsteads of wood are painted green. Each
patient has two sheets, the upper one of which is stitched to the
counterpane. The heating of the wards in winter and the
ventilation at all times are excellently managed . . . we found
everything in the cleanest and best order . . . The Military
Hospital is a splendid establishment. It does the highest honour
to the Empire and to all those concerned in its direction. The
cost per patient is little more than half of the Civil Hospitals –
10 to 12 kopeks per day.[62, 63]

That Tsar Alexander took a very personal interest in the hospitals,
established by Wylie on his orders, is proved by Doctor Robert Lyall,
who had come to St Petersburg to be the physician of the Countess
Orlof Tchésmenska, one of the maids of honour to the empress. He
describes how:

The Emperor may be seen in summer riding in a one-horse
droshki, and in winter in a one-horse sledge, or walking on the
quays of the Neva, or the boulevard of the admiralty in the most
simple uniform. I shall never forget the first time I saw His
Majesty. A few days after his return from Paris in 1815, I was
introduced to Sir James Wylie, with whom I visited some of the
military hospitals at Petersburg, and in which I spoke with a
number of medical gentlemen. A few days afterwards, on the
palace-quay, at no great distance from one of these hospitals, I
remarked an officer in a plain uniform without epaulets, whom I
took for one of the physicians I had seen, and meant to address

him. But for my want of knowledge of the French language, at that time, I should have addressed him. While I hesitated to say *Comment vous portez vous Monsier le Docteur*, or simply, *Docteur?* the Emperor came upon me and stared. I detected my error and passed by. But what was my astonishment at seeing a number of persons, one after the other, standing to one side and taking off their hats as the said officer proceeded forward. On enquiry, I found I had taken the Emperor for a doctor.[64]

Lyall later described how the emperor sometimes visited hospitals totally unannounced:

On his arrival at a town, as soon as time permits, Alexander visits and examines the state of the public institutions and the hospitals, especially the military hospitals, with the minutest attention. Indeed so quick is His Majesty in his motions to these places that he sometimes arrives unexpectedly at an earlier hour than looked for and finds the establishment in its real state.[65]

Much as Russian doctors respected him it was Doctor Lefèvre, physician to the British Embassy in Moscow, who gave the most lasting testimony to Wylie's achievements.

It is to Sir James Wylie that Russia is indebted for the organization of her medical schools both civil and military, and it has been by his persevering industry that the Medical Academy of Petersburg and Moscow has arrived at the honourable rank which it now holds among medical institutions . . . The common soldier has to thank Sir James Wylie for such care and protection as his predecessors demanded in vain and the army in general has to thank him for a real and effective, instead of nominal and inefficient, medical staff.[66]

It was not, in fact, until 1840, on the anniversary of the battle of Borodino, that Tsar Nicholas, the brother who succeeded Alexander, made official recognition of Wylie's service to his country, by ordering the striking of a medal with his portrait on one side. This, although greatly gratifying, did not mean as much to him as a personal letter from Tsar Nicholas. 'You yourself ceased not to give a grand example of zeal and self-denial for the welfare and relief of the suffering warriors.'[67]

Wylie, on receiving this, felt that his moment had arrived.

CHAPTER TWENTY-FOUR

The Military Settlements

Wylie was now to become involved in yet another of Alexander's initiative schemes. The end of the war with France brought new problems of its own. 'The Russian army,' wrote De Maistre, the Sardinian ambassador to Russia, in January 1816, 'consists of 560,000 effective men, and 260,000 reserve'. The plan was to reduce it to 200,000 men, but the question then being asked was how could the soldiers who, once demobilized became free men, find employment in a country where serf labour was the rule?

Shortly after his return to his homeland, the tsar appointed General Alexei Arakcheev as his deputy on the committee of ministers with responsibility for supervising the Committee's decisions and reporting them back to the tsar.

Arakcheev, the Gatchina sergeant-major who had defended Alexander from the tyranny of his father was, as he now realized, totally and unequivocally loyal. He was also ruthlessly efficient. It was largely thanks to him that the ruined city of Smolensk was rebuilt. These were his best qualities. He remained, as he had always been, a cruel and callous man. His temper – and likewise his appearance – had not improved with age. One of his officers described him as having 'cold colourless eyes, a thick and very inelegant nose shaped like a shoe, a rather long chin and tightly compressed lips on which no one could remember having seen a smile or a laugh'.[68]

It was Arakcheev, rather than Wylie, who took credit for the military settlements with which both were closely involved.[69] Alexander first mooted the proposal to establish them in a manifesto of November 1814.

The harsh conditions under which his soldiers were forced to serve had long distressed the tsar. There being no regular conscription, the government ordered the landowners to supply serfs for the army whenever the need arose. The term, which was supposed to last for twenty-five years, in fact continued in most cases until the men were either too old or too ill to fight. Once forced into the army the soldier said farewell to his family, knowing that in all probability he would never see them again. There was no leave, even in peacetime. Neither was there any form of pension either for the men themselves or for their families in the event of them being wounded or killed.

Determined to abolish such injustice, Alexander visualized a plan by which soldiers, in time of peace, could return to their families and work the land allotted to them. However, Arakcheev, when appointed commander-in-chief of all the military settlements in Russia, entirely disregarded the tsar's humane intentions. Peasants, some only boys, forced into uniform, were marched to their work in the fields. At home, in the little huts, women had to have so many pots and platters laid out on a shelf for inspection. Fined for ridiculous irregularities, such as feeding the family fish on a day decreed for soup, or for failing to do washing on a Monday, they were brought before a military tribunal. Men at eighteen and girls at sixteen were married by drawing lots and widows of a child-bearing age were forced to re-marry.

Alexander remained in ignorance of the way in which his benevolent intentions were being carried out. His visits to the military settlements, always known in advance, were arranged so that he departed confident of happy and well-ordered villages.

Famously, on one tour of inspection, with Arakcheev at his side, as he visited every house of a settlement, he found a dinner prepared containing a succulent-looking roast pig. Prince Pyotr Volkonsky, the tsar's aide-de-camp, becoming suspicious, surreptitiously cut the tail off the pig and put it into his pocket. Sure enough, at the next house, there again was the pig, this time minus its tail.

'I think this is an old friend,' Volkonsky said jokingly as he took the tail out of his pocket and put it back beside the end of the pig. But such was the general's hold over Alexander that Volkonsky soon found himself disgraced.

Much enthused with his project, Alexander planned further military establishments on the River Volkhov, near Novgorod and Pskov, and also in the Ukraine. The result was that over 100 infantry battalions and about two hundred squadrons of cavalry, over 750,000 people in all, were planted in these settlements, which included both schools and hospitals.

In charge of the latter buildings was Sir James Wylie who, now in his late fifties, faced yet another enormous task. The fact that so little has been written about his efficiency in accomplishing what would have been a daunting challenge for many a younger man must be put down to the jealousy of his fellow doctors and of the higher echelons of the army of which Arakcheev, with his extraordinary hold over the tsar, was certainly one. It is fair to say that full recognition of Wylie's achievements, in providing well-run hospitals for the Russian soldier and his dependants, was only accorded to him nearly forty years later. It was Nicholas, the brother who succeeded Alexander, who finally gave Wylie the credit for transforming Russian military hospitals, which, although still primitive by modern standards, compared favourably with others of their time.

CHAPTER TWENTY-FIVE

Wrestling with Devils

In the spring of 1818 Alexander set off from Warsaw, where he had been attending an assembly of the Diet, as the Polish parliament was called, to visit the southern provinces of the enormous realm over which he ruled. With him, as part of his entourage, went Wylie, whose professional services were called upon when, on the appallingly bad roads of the country of the Don Cossacks, Alexander's carriage overturned and his leg was badly injured. Wylie insisted that he must take at least a week's rest with the limb in a horizontal position. Alexander, however, with typical stubbornness, would have none of it. His planned curriculum was all-important. Riding and walking, he carried on.

Crossing the estuary of the Don from Azov, he reached the port of Taganrog, which was later to be the scene of dramatic and tragic events. The reason for the tsar's visit in this instance was that he had been advised to demolish the town on the grounds that either Theodosia or Kaffa were better situated as commercial seaports. Alexander, however, on reaching Taganrog, was so impressed by its obvious prosperity and the attractive appearance of the white-walled Tartar houses which clustered round the harbour – claimed to be shallow enough to freeze during the winter months – that he refused to consent to its abolition. In retrospect it would seem that it was the tranquillity and remoteness of this little town which so attracted his restless spirit that it drew him, as irresistibly as a siren, to the danger lying hidden within the surrounding marshes.

Alexander, having toured the southern provinces, eventually returned to St Petersburg after a journey of over 2,000 miles. By then, as Wylie had warned him, the injury to his leg had developed into chronic erysipelas and he also suffered severely from aching at the back of his head.

Wylie now had the tsar's health, both mental and physical, continuously on his mind. Since his return to Russia Alexander had become increasingly neurotic. Obsessed with religion and prone to bouts of depression, he also became convinced that soon he would share the savage fate of his father and grandfather.

The man who had loved to walk among his people now refused to leave the palace until his guards had searched both sides of the street. His paranoia, brought on by overwork and the strain of responsibility of his enormous empire, rapidly and inexorably increased. Wylie did what he could to help him with the medicines available: opium and its derivative laudanum, which was generally mixed with wine, being the main means of killing pain and soothing a troubled mind.

Alexander was also obsessed with the idea of an impending revolution, writing to De Noailles, the French ambassador in St Petersburg, *'Il ne faudra pas que votre gouvernement affranche de la surveillance des armées alliées, s'endrome sur ces dangers'* (It will be important, once your government is freed from the surveillance of the allied armies, that it doesn't ignore these dangers.).[70] De Noailles replied that he believed his government was strong enough to dispel any revolutionary uprising, whereupon Alexander explained to him that the devil was waiting with a powerful secret organization, sworn to death and destruction, which would descend upon Europe. 'We are all prepared for the battle,' Alexander announced.

He was certainly correct in believing that many of Napoleon's supporters continued to plot the assassination of those rulers concerned with his fall. In Paris the Duke of Wellington was fortunate to survive an attack by a man named Cantillon who, when acquitted through the connivance of French agents, was awarded by Napoleon with a legacy for the rest of his life.

Later it was to transpire that a plot had been hatched to seize Tsar Alexander by cutting the traces of his horses when he arrived on the French frontier to visit his army of occupation after leaving the Congress of Aix-la-Chapelle in the autumn of 1818. Once in their hands they were to force him, under pain of death, to sign a paper ordering the liberation of Napoleon and the installation of Napoleon's son as Emperor of France, with his mother Marie Louise as regent.

The insurgents were rumoured to have numbered as many as 1,600 men, including some actually present in Aix-la-Chapelle. However, the strict security measures taken by the Duke of Wellington who, together with Castlereagh and Canning, represented Britain at the Congress, succeeded in foiling their intentions.

When the treaty for the immediate evacuation of France was signed, Alexander went for a single day to Paris to present it to King Louis. The old man, overwhelmed with delight at the gesture (Alexander had travelled nearly 400 miles), afterwards declared that it had been 'one of the happiest moments of my life'.[71]

Having reviewed his army at Valenciennes, Alexander returned to Aix-la-Chapelle, arriving in the middle of the night. The next morning he breakfasted with Wellington and, having thanked him for the care of his troops under his command, he gave him the baton of a Russian field marshal.

The tsar was back in St Petersburg in time to celebrate the Russian New Year of 1819. He was seen to be in excellent spirits and the omens seemed good for the coming year. Then suddenly devastation struck. Catherine Pavlovna, his favourite sister, remarried to Prince William of Württemberg just two years before, suddenly died. Alexander, who had visited her at Stuttgart only the previous month, found it almost impossible to believe. Although an attack of erysipelas in her head was given out as the cause of death, rumours that she had been murdered began to be whispered in the court. Catherine, so vibrant and outspoken, had made enemies – she was known to have quarrelled with her husband's younger brother – but from the little evidence remaining it would seem that pneumonia, resulting from influenza, was the most likely cause of her death.

CHAPTER TWENTY-SIX

Dark Shadow Over the Sun

In the spring of 1819 Tsar Alexander was off again, first to visit Finland and then to the Russian port of Archangel. On the journey, while crossing a lake in a ferry boat, he survived a violent storm. To Wylie, who was with him, it must have seemed providential that now, for the second time in his life, just as when he had tried as a boy to escape by sea in the little brig lying in the harbour at Cramond, he again escaped being drowned.

In Archangel, with Wylie in attendance, Alexander minutely inspected both the hospitals and the prisons. Then, after making the long journey south to Krasnoe Selo, he watched the annual manoeuvres of his army taking place on the wide surrounding plain.

His brother Nicholas was there with his army brigade. Nicholas had married Princess Alexandra Feodorovna, daughter of King Frederick William of Prussia and his wife Queen Louise, whom Alexander had so dearly loved. She wrote of how they were both taken aback when, one night at dinner, Alexander suddenly said 'that he was doubly pleased to see Nicholas carry out his duties so well because on him would fall one day a heavy weight of responsibility'.

He looked on him [Nicholas] as the person who would replace him; and this would happen much sooner than anyone imagined, since it would occur while he himself was still alive. We sat there like two statues, open-eyed and dumb. The Emperor went on, 'you seem astonished, but let me tell you that my brother Constantine, who has never bothered about the throne, is more than ever determined to renounce it formally and to pass on his rights to his brother Nicholas and his descendants. As for myself I have decided to free myself of my functions and to retire from the world . . . I am no longer the man I was, and I think it is my duty to retire in good time' . . . Seeing us on the verge of tears he tried to comfort us and reassure us by saying that this was not going to happen at once, that some years must pass before he carried out his plan.[72]

The tsar was in St Petersburg when, in June 1819, the soldiers and peasants in a military colony in the Ukraine rebelled against the harsh discipline they received. General Arakcheev at once travelled down there and punished the leaders of the revolt with terrible floggings, which frequently ended in their death.

Alexander supported him officially although inwardly greatly disturbed. Aware that there were secret societies, many of them Masonic in origin, he refused to interfere with their liberal beliefs. To the governor-general of St Petersburg, who urged him to prohibit the secret societies in the city, he merely replied, 'You know that I have shared and encouraged these illusions and errors. It is not for me to deal severely with them.'[73]

Sometimes Alexander suggested he might abdicate but without any clear indication of when this was to take place. A short time after talking to Nicholas and Alexandra, either on his journey to Finland or on the way back, he met Julie von Krüdner again in a church in the small town of Pechory in Estonia. There she told him that the King of Prussia's life was in danger unless he gave himself up entirely to God and that the Holy Alliance must be continued to confront the evils of the world.

In August 1819 Alexander, again with Wylie in attendance, went to Riga where a deputation was presented to him with a scheme for emancipation. The tsar congratulated the envoys, telling them that they had set an example that ought to be imitated, and that they had 'acted in the spirit of our age'. From Riga he continued to Mittau to attend the ceremonies involving the enfranchisement of the serfs of Courland. Then, as usual in September, wearing the Polish uniform and the white eagle, he attended the Diet in Warsaw, where the city was illuminated in his honour.

The baroness's predictions seemed to be coming true as rebellions against the government broke out in both Spain and Naples. In London a plot to assassinate the cabinet was foiled but in France the

Duc de Berri, nephew of Louis XVIII, was murdered. Metternich then instigated a meeting at Troppau (Opava), the capital of Austrian Silesia, between the emperors of Russia and Austria to discuss methods of counteracting the threat of revolution facing Europe. Metternich, determined to force Russia and Austria to collaborate, largely succeeded in his aims when Alexander offered an army 100,000 strong to help subdue the insurgents in southern Italy. With him at the congress was the Grand Duke Nicholas, a further indication of his intention to make him his heir.

Negotiations continued far longer than expected and Alexander was still at Troppau when, on 9 November 1820, a message came from Arakcheev that the Semeonovski regiment had mutinied, Alexander was mortified and also greatly alarmed. Since the time of his father's murder the Semeonovskii had been his special regiment, which he believed to be loyal to the core. 'It is easy for you to imagine the sorrow this has caused me,' he wrote to Arakcheev. 'I think incitement came from outside the army.'

Convinced now of the threat of revolution in his own country Alexander, concurring with Metternich's decision to refuse to receive an emissary from the Neapolitan insurgents, reached agreement with the Austrians and the Prussians to unite against further unrest wherever and whenever it should occur.

The conference adjourned, the tsar returned to St Petersburg where he ordered the rebels to be treated with mercy although the officers were to be cashiered.

The city itself was now in the midst of one of the coldest winters ever known. Starving wolves roamed the streets. After three coachmen were frozen to death Alexander issued a decree prohibiting evening entertainments in St Petersburg when the temperature dropped to seventeen degrees below zero. Yet despite the Arctic conditions Alexander set off for Troppau, where the conference was to resume, in an open sleigh. Wrapped in furs he survived the journey, as did his now aging doctor whose resilience must be marvelled at considering the rigours he endured.

From Troppau Alexander went to the city of Ljubljana (Laibach in German) in what was then Carniola and is now Slovenia. There he heard that the Piedmontese army had mutinied, demanding a war against Austria in support of the Neapolitans. Convinced of his belief that God had sent him there to defend the Austrians, Alexander proclaimed, 'If we save Europe it is because he has desired it', and immediately ordered that 90,000 men be ready to march to Austria's aid.

At Laibach, perhaps due to the cold and the jolting he had endured during the long sleigh journey, Alexander was again laid low with another attack of erysipelas. While there he received a plea from Napoleon's aide Las Casas, begging for Napoleon's release. Alexander officially refused to countenance an arrangement which he rightly believed might threaten the already fragile stability of King Louis. He did, however, suggest through his ambassador that the British government might hold out some hope of the exiled emperor's eventual release, which is said to have raised Napoleon's hopes of freedom. Then, on 5 May 1821, the man once thought to be invincible suddenly and unexpectedly died.

The tsar was still at Laibach when told that one of his own aides-de-camps, Prince Alexander Ypsilantis, had raised a rebellion against the Turkish rulers in the principalities of the Danube. Soon the Greek Christians were fighting the sultan and Ypsilantis made a dramatic appeal to Alexander to 'save our religion from those who would persecute it'. But Alexander's hands were tied. By the terms of the recent congress he had condemned revolution and he now promised Metternich that he would not interfere in the Balkan conflict, thus assuring Ypsilantis' defeat.

Alexander returned to St Petersburg a tired and worried man. The war in the Balkans was escalating. Appalling atrocities, committed on both sides, included the execution of the Greek Patriarch Gregorios outside his own palace in Constantinople.

Monsieur Dupré de St Maur, an official in the imperial household, was among those who noticed the tsar's obvious despondency. 'I do not know if I deceive myself, but I frequently observe in Alexander's features a sad and painfully occupied expression. If I meet him on the high road when alone in his carriage and he does not try to compose his face, I recognize that same expression. How many times I have said to my wife, "I have just seen the

Emperor. Ah! What shadows and uneasiness there were on his brow!" '74

Depressed and stricken with remorse at his inability to help those of his own faith, Alexander, through his friend Prince Golitsyn, arranged another meeting with the mysterious Baroness von Krüdner. They met in a peasant's house by the road to Tsarskoe Selo. No record remains of their conversation although it is known that the baroness publicly announced that Alexander would be in Constantinople by the year 1823. It proved to be their last meeting. Having pestered him with a long written screed in which she ordered him to lead a campaign against the Turkish infidels, she disappeared to Latvia, whence she never returned.

Alexander attended, two more conferences, in Vienna and then in Verona, in the following year of 1822. At the latter event he recovered some of his former love of entertainment as he attended a banquet and an opera by Rossini, conducted by the great composer himself. Again he noticed pretty women. He was seen to flirt with Lady Londonderry and, on a more serious note, to converse with the Duke of Wellington, whom he so greatly admired.

Nonetheless, despite his public appearance, he was secretly beset with terror at the sight of the milling crowds. Later, in the Crimea, Sir James Wylie was to tell Doctor Robert Lee that while they were in Verona 'so great was the Emperor's fear of assassination by the Carbonari that he durst not venture into the streets until they had been inspected by guards sent out for that purpose, and that this dread even prevented His Majesty from going to Rome, which he had a great desire to visit'.[75]

Lee was also told by the Belgian diplomat, Count Caraman, that:

> While at Verona he had often taken long walks with the Emperor into the surrounding country and that he was then affected by an unaccountable gloom and melancholy, and believed that he was destined to be miserable and unfortunate. He conceived that this feeling, with the horrible attack meditated on his life, reduced him to a state of utter despair, and rendered him anxious not to live, and induced him to refuse all help.

Wylie alone knew the reason for his paranoia, but others who had known him beforehand noticed the sadness in his face. To the Emperor Francis he confided that he knew he was soon to die, and to the Quaker William Allen, a friend from his time in England, he poured out all his troubles, telling him that 'he felt himself so weak he dared not look far ahead'.[76]

CHAPTER TWENTY-SEVEN

The Toll of Long Travel

Returning to St Petersburg, depressed and restless as ever, the tsar again began travelling, always at a furious pace. In an open carriage, accompanied only by Wylie, two equerries and a valet, his horses pulled him at a reckless rate, north and south, east and west, over Russia's vast distances.

Refusing to hold any formal receptions, and avoiding the palaces of the nobility, he stopped instead by the wayside to chat with the peasants, asking about their crops and animals and sometimes going into their cottages or to the local churches to talk to the parish priests.

During the following summer Alexander went to watch the manoeuvres near Grodno. An officer lost control of his horse, which reared and then lashed out suddenly, striking the tsar on the left leg. Wincing with pain he was helped to dismount, and although the bone was discovered not to be broken, he was very badly bruised.

Travelling back to St Petersburg the tsar made a brief visit to Moscow where the crowds surged round his carriage, calling him their 'little father' and waiting just to catch a glimpse of him in a deluge of icy rain. But on receiving a message that Elizabeth was far from well, he went rushing back to St Petersburg again with all possible speed.

Alexander found her looking drawn and tired, coughing constantly from an infection in her lungs. Elizabeth now looked an old woman although she was only forty-five. Gone was the near ethereal beauty, the shining hair and the fair complexion. The court gossips made the most of her illness, claiming that, as had happened on previous occasions, Alexander was looking elsewhere. But instead their love for each other was rekindled. The bond between them strengthened as Alexander realized the true worth of the wife to whom he had so often been unfaithful but whose love for him had never changed.

At Epiphany, on 6 January, while forbidding the usual escort of guards to be exposed to the freezing weather, the tsar himself stood on the palace's Jordan Staircase bareheaded and without gloves while prayers were chanted by the Metropolitan for nearly half an hour. Three of his fingers were frostbitten and had to be rubbed with snow before he returned to the Winter Palace, shivering and blue with cold.

Such was the intensity of the weather that one young courtier actually died of hypothermia. Alexander himself was plainly unwell, but a few days later insisted on going to Tsarskoe Selo over roads packed hard with snow. There, while he was taking his usual morning walk, he was caught in a snowstorm and returned to the palace soaked through. Soon he became feverish and delirious as the dreaded scourge of erysipelas spread over his body and into his head.

His illness at this point, however unlikely, is claimed to have saved his life, for he was due to have gone to Belaia Tserkov to review the troops stationed there. Had he done so he would have stayed in a small isolated house in a park where some officers, disguised as ordinary soldiers, planned to strangle him before raising a rebellion throughout the empire.

At Tsarskoe Selo, however, he became so ill that Wylie insisted he return to the Winter Palace in a carriage with a closed roof.

Now it was Elizabeth who nursed him as his left leg, damaged already by the horse's kick, and hurt again by a fall on the Winter Palace stairs, became red and swollen as the erysipelas returned. In Vienna, where Wylie had treated it successfully with iced water, the affliction had been confined to his limb, but now it spread across much of his body. His leg began to turn black and gangrene became recognizable by its noxious smell.

The doctors, summoned to attend him, wanted to amputate below the knee. But Wylie, who remained in charge as his personal physician, warning that if the tsar died they would be held responsible, used his authority to prevent the operation taking place. Defying the outspoken doubt and antagonism of his colleagues, he then bled the tsar and cauterised the morbid flesh.

The city shrank into silence as news of the emperor's illness spread. Theatres were empty, balls were cancelled, and the crowds outside the palace waited in silent dread. People prayed in the churches throughout the day and night and, as a French governess wrote, even beggars found coppers to light candles to pray for the emperor's recovery.

Meanwhile, within the palace itself, Alexander was given little peace as his mother, the bustling, imperious Maria Feodorovna, and his brothers, Nicholas and Michael, the latter soon to be married to Princess Helen of Württemberg, came morning and night to visit him. Finally Wylie, finding Alexander's temperature to have risen, lost his usually cool reserve and ordered them all out of the room. The dowager empress, much affronted, began to expostulate whereupon Elizabeth, for so long the downtrodden daughter-in-law, turned on her and asked her quite bluntly whether she wanted her son to die. Maria, shocked into silence, then left without a word, while the grand dukes Nicholas and Michael actually crept on tip-toe down the stairs.

For some days the crisis continued but then, as the fever abated, Alexander appeared to be on the mend. Wylie placed him on a vegetarian diet until, to the amazement of the other physicians, who had forecast his imminent death, the tsar began to regain his normal state of health. So quickly did he recover that by the end of March, he and Elizabeth, with Wylie as ever in attendance, moved to Tsarskoye Selo. There in the country, fifteen miles from St Petersburg and free from the rest of his family, he was able to continue his convalescence in peace.

The Alexander Palace, or as it was more commonly known the Great Palace, with its great front and two wings, had been given to Alexander by his grandmother, Catherine the Great, on his marriage. The north part, which had burned down, had by then been rebuilt. Within the chapel, the columns and pilasters were almost entirely covered in gold and beautiful paintings hung from the walls.

Here, in a four-storeyed wing of the neoclassical building designed by Vasily Stasov, Alexander had established a college, the Tsarskoye Selo Lyceum, in 1811. Intended for the education of landowners' sons, one of its first graduates had been Alexander Pushkin, famed throughout Russia as a poet, novelist and social reformer. Recently arrested by the authorities in Odessa, he was actually living in exile on his mother's estate in Estonia at the time of the founder's visit to his former academy.

Rather than stay in the vast building, now occupied by noisy students, Alexander and Elizabeth chose to occupy part of the adjacent, even more architecturally impressive Catherine Palace, so named because it had been built by Peter the Great for his wife Catherine in 1717. Following her death it had become the favourite summer home of their daughter, the Empress Elizabeth, who in 1743 had commissioned the great Italian architect Bartolomeo Rastrelli to completely redesign the building in a style as resplendent as Versailles.

The result was a palace, nearly a kilometre in circumference, fronted with decorated blue and white facades featuring gilded atlantes, caryatids and pilasters designed by the German sculptor Johann Franz Dunker, who, on the outside of the building alone, used over 220 pounds of gold. The rooms within the palace were no less ornate than the exterior, the golden enfilade of the state rooms, designed by Rastrelli, being the most outstanding feature of all. The Great Hall, stretching the whole width of the palace, with arched windows on either side, is aptly called the Hall of Light. Leading from it, other rooms include the Portrait Hall, the Picture Gallery, crowded with canvasses from floor to ceiling, and most importantly of all, Rastrelli's great masterpiece – famous then as now throughout the world – the Amber Room.

To achieve this the architect used panels of amber mosaic, which had originally been designed for an Amber Cabinet at Königsberg Castle. He then embellished them with gilded carving, mirrors and more panels of amber, created by craftsmen from Florence and Russia, inset with mosaics of gemstones from the Urals and the Caucasus, creating one of the most astonishing of all the beautiful rooms in the many palaces in Russia.

Alexander was at home in the Catherine Palace, for it was here that, in his childhood, he and his brother Constantine had spent many happy summers with their grandmother, who so dearly loved both the palace itself and the surrounding gardens.

Once fully recovered from his ailments, Alexander resumed his normal routine of rising at seven, working with secretaries until noon, and then walking in the English Park, so called because it was laid out by the English-trained landscape designer Johann Busch, on the instruction of the Empress Catherine in the 1770s. A central attraction, fringed by overhanging trees, is the meandering lake, or the Great Pond as it was called, where the Dutch-style boathouses were known as the Admiralty, and the Marble Bridge was modelled on those of the great houses of Stowe and Wilton in England.

Elizabeth, walking with him, fed the swans on the pond. Then afterwards he rested while she sat beside him, quietly doing her embroidery and making sure that his sleep was undisturbed. They dined together at four, and after Alexander had attended to any business of importance, she joined him in his study, where, after drinking tea made in a samovar, they spent the rest of the evening quietly together until it was time to go to bed.

It was during this period that Wylie himself had an accident as his own carriage overturned. His injuries are not described in detail but are said to have been serious. More worthy of note was the tsar's great concern for his personal physician, as he sat by his bedside for three whole days until Wylie was out of danger.

Successful as he was, however, in effecting a bodily cure, even Wylie, with all his expertise, could not heal Alexander's mind. At the end of June he went to Krasnoe Selo, about sixteen miles from St Petersburg, where, in Elizabeth's words, the small palace was so dominated by the army that she felt inclined to head her letters, 'From General Headquarters'.[77] On this occasion Alexander, true to form, had gone to watch army manoeuvres. As he mounted his horse he realized that his aides-de-camps were whispering among themselves and guessed they were trying to hide something from him. Turning in his saddle to Wylie, who was standing near him, he asked him bluntly what was happening and Wylie found himself forced to tell him that Sophia, the elder of the two daughters borne him by his Polish mistress Maria Naryshkin, had died of tuberculosis.

The girl had been educated in Paris, purportedly to save Elizabeth the embarrassment of seeing her husband's illegitimate child in the same city where she lived. However, although she was known to be delicate, her ambitious mother insisted on her being brought to Russia to marry Count Shuvalov, one of the tsar's aides-de-camps.

Elizabeth, walking one day in the garden at Krasnoe Selo, met her in the company of the Shuvalovs. Recognizing her immediately she gave her a kiss, saying, 'I cannot help loving you for the likeness you bear; it is impossible to mistake it.' Tragically, it was only a short time afterwards that the girl, who was only eighteen, died of a haemorrhage in her lungs.

As the news was brought to Alexander, the officers standing near him thought for a moment that he was ill. Tears streamed down his face and he sat astride his horse in dumb misery throughout the rest of the parade. Convinced that the death of his daughter was God's punishment for his sins, he was devastated with feelings of guilt and remorse. The affair with Maria was long over and now, in his misery, he turned to his wife for comfort and to his doctor for support.

The year 1817 had seen the reintroduction of a great annual event in the form of a ball or fête at the Winter Palace, with a supper at the Hermitage, an event unique to Russia. All and sundry were invited, peasants and princes alike. Once, according to De Maistre, the guests had even included a Serbian chief, who had murdered both his father and his brother by hanging them with his own hands.[78]

On 13 January 1824 Alexander insisted on being present at this grand annual event. Ignoring a warning that an attempt would be made to assassinate him, he allowed no special precautions to be taken and was reported to be looking more cheerful than usual while a vast concourse of people roamed through the rooms of the Winter Palace.

Nonetheless, despite his apparent nonchalance towards the ever-present threats to his life, none knew better than his doctor the secret and all-pervading anxiety which so constantly obsessed his mind.

CHAPTER TWENTY-EIGHT

The Great Flood

In the autumn Elizabeth returned from visiting her mother in Baden. She wrote how the smell of Russia, 'that dear country', gladdened her heart, but that the sight of the Winter Palace plunged her into depression, as she thought of the tedium of court protocol and more particularly of the dominance of her mother-in-law, behind whom, thanks to a law of Tsar Paul's which gave precedence to the dowager empress, she was still forced to walk on all ceremonial occasions.

Only two days after his return to St Petersburg, Alexander and Elizabeth were together in the Winter Palace when, on the night of 18 November 1824, the wind from the south-west began to rise. By daylight the following day it was blowing a hurricane. The River Neva, running higher than anyone could remember, and combined with an incoming tide which pushed back the water, soon flooded much of the city. Within the palace itself the occupants shivered with cold and fear. Elizabeth, writing to her mother, described how they dared not light the fires in case the chimneys caught alight in the force of the high wind.

A doctor then living in St Petersburg described what had happened in a letter to his friend Doctor Robert Lee:

> I attempted to cross the Voskresensky Bridge of boats, on my way to the General Naval Hospital on the Wybor side, but was unable owing to the great elevation [of the water]. I then paid some professional visits; and at eleven o'clock called on Prince Naryshkin [gentleman-in-waiting to the Empress Elizabeth], who had already given orders to remove the furniture from his lower apartments, the water then being above the level of the Fontanka Canal, opposite to his residence. From this time the rise was rapid; and at half-past eleven, when I returned to my

house, in the great Millione, the water was gushing upwards through the gratings of the sewers, filling the streets and court-yards with which every house is provided. A servant took me on his back from the droshky, my horses at that time being above their knees, and conveyed me to the landing of the staircase. The wind now blew in awful gusts; and the noise of the tempest with the cries of the people in the streets was terrific. It was not long before boats were seen in the streets, with vast quantities of firewood and other articles floating about . . . Now and then a horse was seen swimming across from one pavement to another. The number of rats drowned on this occasion was inconceivable; and of dogs and cats not a few. The crisis seemed to be from one to three in the afternoon, at which hour the wind having veered round a couple of points to the northward, the water began to abate; and by four o'clock the tops of the iron posts, three feet in height, by the sides of the pavement, made their appearance.

From the commencement of the report the signal cannon, fired first at the Galleyhaven at the entrance of the river, then at the Admiralty dockyard, and lastly at the fortress, was continued at intervals as a warning to the inhabitants, and added not a little to the horror of the scene.

The depth of water in the different parts of the city varied from four to nine and ten feet, but along the border of the Gulf of Finland, and especially in the low suburb of the Galleyhaven, the depth was from fourteen to eighteen feet, and many of the small wooden houses built on piles were carried away, inmates and all. A few were floated up the Neva, rocking about with poor creatures clinging on to the roof. Some of these perished; others were taken off at great risk, by boats from the Admiralty yard, which had been ordered out by the express command of his Imperial Majesty, who stood during the greatest part of the day on the balcony of the Winter Palace, giving the necessary orders.

On the 20th, the Emperor Alexander, ever benevolent and humane, visited those parts of the city and suburbs most afflicted by this catastrophe. In person he bestowed alms and consolation to the sufferers, for the most part of the lower classes, and in every way afforded such relief, both then and afterwards, as won for him the still greater love and admiration of his people and of the foreign residents in St Petersburg.

Over 600 people in all are said to have perished in the flood. Hospitals and prisons were evacuated, and according to another account the Winter Palace and other public buildings were opened on the emperor's orders so that people could be saved from the flood. Alexander's youngest sister, the Grand Duchess Anna, now married to William of Orange (William II of the Netherlands) who was visiting her brother, described how 'the square in front of the Winter Palace, the boulevard and the streets which lead to the Palace showed a terrible sight of a raging sea'.

The tsar's sister continued to describe how the next morning he insisted on going out to supervise the relief work. Wading through the mud of the devastated streets – elsewhere it is claimed that he went about rescuing people in a boat – from one of the ruined hovels a voice cried out, 'It is a punishment from God Almighty for our sins!' But Alexander was heard to reply, 'No; it is a punishment for my sin.'

CHAPTER TWENTY-NINE

Taganrog

Alexander was by now visibly unwell. At Epiphany, at the beginning of January in 1824, he stood for hours bareheaded as a hole was bored through the ice and the blessing of the Neva took place. Shivering, he returned to the Winter Palace, where during the evening's festivities he was plainly seen to be ill. Nonetheless he insisted in going to Tsarskoe Selo, driving through drifts of snow.

Then even as the floods subsided, people in St Petersburg began to fall ill. Among them the Empress Elizabeth developed rheumatic fever, which badly affected her heart. Her own physician, Doctor Stoffregen, consulted Wylie who diagnosed her illness as firstly angina pectoris and later tuberculosis, which worsened her already weakened heart.[79] The two physicians, greatly concerned for her, suggested to Alexander that, to escape the cold of St Petersburg, he should take his wife to recuperate in a warmer climate. He then put forward the idea of their going to Taganrog, a port on the Sea of Azov.

This caused great speculation. Why, the courtiers demanded, had Taganrog, of all places, been chosen as a suitable place for the empress, now known by everyone to be in a delicate state of health, to spend the winter? Taganrog was a small seaside port, built originally by Peter the Great on a site near the mouth of the River Don. It was not thought particularly healthy, there being river mashes nearby, and moreover it was well known to be prone to gales sweeping northwards across the Sea of Azov. Why, people asked, did they not go to the Crimea? There were some beautiful villas in Yalta, greatly superior to the Tartar houses in Taganrog. Why did the emperor not rent one of them? Moreover the climate there was warmer, so mild in fact that palms and semi-tropical plants flourished in profusion on the shores. No one, it seems, remembered that Crimean fever was endemic, although at the time it had yet to be discovered that mosquitoes were the carriers of the disease.

Whatever the arguments against Taganrog, the tsar would not be moved. His decision to go there has since prompted much conjecture that the real reason for choosing Taganrog was that it was a port where it would be easy to find a ship on which to slip out to sea unseen. At the time it was merely presumed that the tsar, who was known to be preoccupied with mysticism, was seeking a remote area where, for a time at least, he and the Empress Elizabeth, also known to hate public events, could live in seclusion, undisturbed.

The decision now reached, couriers were despatched immediately to find a suitable house in Taganrog. The little town, which then had about 8,000 or 9,000 inhabitants, stands on a promontory, from where, in the distance, the mountains of the Caucasus rear against the sky. To the east lies a bay, some distance from the mouth of the Don.

A house with eleven bedrooms, some of them with views over the sea, was found, and although rather small, it was considered suitable for the royal couple to rent. A visitor in 1890, calling it 'the palace in Taganrog' described it as it was then, apparently little changed from the time of Alexander and Elizabeth's occupation sixty-five years before:

> The palace in Taganrog consists of a small one-storey building. It has 13 windows facing the street; on the right is the gate which leads into the courtyard with a porch and an outhouse; there is a small garden on the left-hand side. The façade is painted in yellow ochre, its decorations are painted white; the roof supposedly was green. In general, the quite modest appearance of the building does not make it look like a palace.[80]

A string of wagons left St Petersburg for Taganrog, all of them loaded according to lists drawn up by Alexander himself. Curtains, carpets, beds and furniture, even the accoutrements of a chapel, china, silver, glass and ornaments were trundled down the length of Russia to the Sea of Azov in the south. Over and above this, every single stage of his wife's journey was provided for by her husband including special pillow cases, candle shades, and even Dresden china for her breakfast and her tea. Elizabeth wrote to her mother, saying she was deeply touched by Alexander's solicitude for her comfort. So worried was he, in fact, that no fewer than five doctors travelled with them, but it was only Wylie who, together with two aides-de camps, went on ahead of the empress with Alexander himself.

Before leaving St Petersburg Alexander interviewed all his ministers and wound up the affairs of state with the thoroughness for which he was renowned. On the evening of his departure he dined with his two brothers, Nicholas and Michael. 'It was here,' wrote Nicholas afterwards, 'that he bade farewell to him for whom he ever cherished a sentiment of the deepest and most affectionate gratitude, and also to the Empress Elizabeth.'

Again with his extraordinary energy, Alexander was up at four o'clock the next morning to go alone, in the dark, to a service for the dead in the Alexander Nevsky Monastery. Afterwards he was closeted for some time in the cell of a celebrated hermit who had recently arrived in St Petersburg.

Leaving the church, and joined by Doctor Wylie and the two aides-de-camps who were to travel with him, he headed for Tsarskoye Selo to say goodbye to his mother and sisters. Day had now dawned and on a piece of high ground he ordered his coachmen to rein in the horses. Through gaps in the trees, as he looked back at St Petersburg, he could see the familiar view of the gilded spires and domes rising above the Neva, before the distant rim of the sea, shining clear in the morning light. Afterwards his faithful driver was to say that it had seemed as though he was committing to memory the great city of his realm.

CHAPTER THIRTY

The Doctor's Diaries

First-hand accounts of the calamitous and historic incidents which took place in Russia from the autumn of 1825 until the following spring, are revealed by the diary kept by Sir James Wylie, and the journal of his fellow physician Doctor Robert Lee.

Wylie was mostly concerned with the state of the emperor's health. Lee, on the other hand, wrote a vivid description of the Crimea, through which he was travelling just before and after Alexander and Wylie arrived at Taganrog.

Lee, after graduating at Edinburgh University, had led a varied and in many ways strange career. After working for one year in a country practice and two in Edinburgh hospitals he had, through the influence of the famous Sir Gilbert Blane, gone down to England to look after the epileptic son of William Lamb and his notoriously eccentric wife, Lady Caroline. After five unhappy years in that disordered household, he had managed to escape to Paris, where, after spending some time in improving his knowledge of anatomy in the dissecting rooms and clinics of the city, he had become doctor to the Bessborough family. Then, in 1824, when he was still only thirty-one, he had become personal physician to no less a person than Count Michael Vorontzov, Governor General of South Russia. Travelling across Europe from Paris he had finally reached the Ukrainian capital Odessa. The city, founded by Prince Potemkin, uncrowned emperor of South Russia, remained in a state of development. The palace of the Vorontzovs was not yet even finished, which meant that Lee had to live with the family in a house nearby.

Arriving in Odessa he had at first got the impression that society there was as free and easy as in London. But after some time, becoming suspicious, he had discovered that a plot was afoot to destroy the Emperor Alexander and subvert the government of the country. Intrigued, and slightly apprehensive, he had then been made aware of the powerful network of detection, organized to counteract subversion when, at a public ball, after he had been talking to Count de Witt, Prince Serge Volkonsky had tapped him on the shoulder and whispered in his ear 'take care what you say, he is the emperor's spy'.

Lee claimed that 'the army is rotten to the core. Many of the officers detest the present system of government . . . and long to see the slaves educated and gradually emancipated.' He then forecast, with remarkable accuracy, that the revolution, which he rightly believed to be inevitable, would begin in the ranks of the army.

That Alexander himself was aware of the unrest within Russia is clear from all contemporary accounts. It is also known, from his own words, that the weight of the responsibility that had been his since the death of his father twenty-four years before, was becoming almost more than he could endure. A main reason for going to Taganrog, in addition to Elizabeth's frail health, must have been to escape for a time the constant demands put upon him in St Petersburg, if not perhaps forever.

Wylie, perhaps secretly, did keep a diary, jotting down the details of his visit with Alexander to Taganrog in that fateful autumn of 1825. His dates are those of the Julian calendar rather than the Gregorian, which although by then commonly used in Britain, was not to be accepted in Russia until 1918.

From what he writes it would seem that Alexander made a diversion into Poland before heading south. Historians have since considered it significant that Wylie describes their arrival at Taganrog as the end of 'the first part of their journey'. Presumably it can be taken that by then he knew of Alexander's intention to visit the Crimea – or can it be surmised that he was already party to a plot by which, in this remote location, the tsar meant to stage his disappearance? Wylie begins his diary on 1 September 1825.

The leaves have started fading and falling, the grass has grown yellow; the morning was cold, the weather was beautiful. Like migrating birds we set off on our flight – the time has come for us to depart, in order to find a warmer climate. His Majesty approved of the list of medicines.

As was usual with Alexander, he travelled at a hectic speed. Details of the journey from the edge of the Baltic to the shore of the Sea of Azov, which drains into the Black Sea, noted by Wylie in his diary, show how it affected them both.

September 5th. We arrived at Dorogobuzh [about 50 m. E. of Smolensk] quite late; my ill health still persists; good weather holds; the roads are dry and wonderful. His Majesty assured me yesterday that he did not feel the slightest pain in his leg. This town trades mostly with Riga.

6th. Everything goes perfectly: the weather, the road. The horses agree with our wishes. Conversation today turned around political economy. Here we are entering the domain of Repnin.

7th. The weather has changed: it has become foggy and rainy. On my arrival I found 12 patients left in the hospital of the Sixth Division, they are very ill but on the other hand well kept. Doctor Korbov (22nd Infantry) is good.

8th. The roads are rather rough and the weather is rainy: today we spent the whole time in Novgorod,[81] a market town, an unimportant place.

9th. The hospital in Sherbury(?) is in a good situation; the eparch served wonderfully in the cathedral; the weather has improved: the roads in the Orel and Kursk Governments are far superior to those in Chernigov.

10th. Spent the night at Bogatoye [about 50 m. E. of Kuyby-shev]. Duca's people were present. I saw Bibikov. From there we headed for Chuguyev [approx. 25 m. S.E. of Kharkoy].

11th. We are in Chuguyev, in the palace. Leontovich and Shivanov arrived from Kharkov. The hospital is too far from the water, the windows are too high, the building has no eaves-troughs; the patient care is poor.

Travelling through the Ukraine the tsar saw for himself how the peasants were suffering due to locusts ravaging the land. Despite an exceptionally cold winter, when the Black Sea had frozen so hard that Constantinople and the Mediterranean had been cut off from all forms of shipping, the whole of the district, between the great rivers of the Danube and the Dniester, was over-run by these pests. By now they were spreading from beyond the Dnieper and the Don into the Caucasus. There were millions of them, said to move with the south wind only in the light of day. Doctor Robert Lee, who two months earlier, in July, had travelled from Kiev to Odessa, describes how:

> They rose as our carriages approached, with a peculiar rattling noise, and in such number that they filled the air like flakes of snow in a storm. They swarmed in the streets of Odessa, in the vineyards and on the surrounding steppe, at the beginning of August, and masses of the dead bodies of those drowned in the sea covered the shore.

Everywhere peasants were working frantically, trying to destroy the pests. Gangs of men were digging ditches, hoping to control their advance. Lined up above were children, waiting to catch and destroy any insects that tried to crawl up the sides. Deep holes were dug in the trenches into which the locusts were swept before slaves shovelled them into sacks with wooden spades. Doctor Lee was distressed by the plight of the people of these areas.

> A more wretched, ill-clothed, miserable race, I never saw; lodging in holes in the ground, worse covered than our common vagrants and beggars, and men behind them with whips which I saw used.[82]

In the Ukraine, at least in the summer months, the peasants simply lay down to sleep in the fields once their work was done. Across the steppes, however, came roaming bands of Tartars, proud, dark-skinned men in robes, their hair concealed by turbans, riding ponies with the ease of born horsemen. Their women and children travelled in wagons, which they drew up at night to form squares, the drivers sitting round their fires in the centre while the oxen grazed outside.

Returning to Odessa Lee then sailed with Count Vorontsov and his suite on Admiral Greig's yacht to the Crimea. Aleksey Samuilovich Greig, an Admiral of the Imperial Russian Navy, was a son of the famous Samuel Greig, who, coming from Inverkeithing in Fife, had been appointed by Catherine the Great as commander of her famous navy. The son, so like him in appearance, was commander of the Black Sea Fleet and Military Governor of Sevastopol and Nikolayev. Also on board was Count Fyodor Pahlen, son of the organizer of Tsar Paul's murder, now Plenipotentiary President of the Divans in the Danube principalities.

Having crossed the Black Sea to Sevastopol, Lee with several companions took leave of the admiral and sailed for Yoursouff, the seat of Count Vorontsov, on the south coast of the Crimea.

There, in the very south of the Crimea, they found themselves in what Lee describes as 'a terrestrial paradise. The weather was delightful. There were none of the sudden and violent changes which happened so frequently in the countries lying to the north of the Black Sea'. Yet despite the near perfect climate the country was rampant with disease.

> During the month of September 1825, the whole population of the Crimea between the mountains and the sea, all the inhabitants of this 'terrestrial paradise', were in a very sickly condition, and in the villages along the coast between Yoursouff and Simeiz, I saw and treated more than a hundred cases of intermittent and remittent fever. Many who had been suffering for months had enlargement of the liver and spleen, with jaundice and dropsy . . . There could be little doubt that the fever which then prevailed on the coast and in the interior of the Crimea was produced by noxious exhalations from the earth.

Alexander reached Taganrog on 14 September 1825 (Julian calendar). Elizabeth had travelled more slowly over mainly country roads and Alexander met her carriage at the last coaching station before Taganrog. The house, so carefully prepared for her, filled her immediately with joy. The terrace, the small garden, the apricot trees in the garden, the changing colours of the sea, all seemed perfect in her eyes. Moreover, away from his family, she now had Alexander to herself. Together they drove in a carriage, exploring the roads by the sea and the surrounding country with its plantations and cornfields which lay near the sea below the great stretches of the steppes. In the town itself, an estimated population of 7,600 people, of which two-thirds were Greek, nearly doubled as ships arrived during the summer months. The broad streets were unpaved, and the houses with their brightly painted walls were built of both stone and wood. Here they spoke to local people, and bought trinkets in the shops run by the Tartars and the Jews who comprised most of the population of the little town.

Doctor Lee, describing Taganrog, wrote that the streets were wide and clean, and the pavements high and paved with hard stones brought from the seashore, and lit by lamps at night. Each house had a courtyard, surrounded by a number of huts for servants and labourers. The courts, however,

> Usually presented a scene of filth and confusion which baffles all description; only surpassed by some of the trackers in Poland. Here are seen standing a number of old droshkies, caleches, carts and barrels upon wheels for bringing water, all up to the axletrees in mud, and exposed to the general influence of this rude climate. Before the Emperor came here I was informed that the town was as dirty and neglected as any town in Russia. A law was then passed by the town council, imposing a tax of thirty kopeks on each cart that goes with corn, or any kind of commodity, to the port, or in lieu of this, the cart must return loaded with stones from the sea-shore for the streets. This law has had the effect of rendering the streets very good – much superior to those in Odessa.

Wylie's diary, written in Taganrog, continues to describe how there followed several days of good weather until, as it began to change, a comet, thought to presage disaster, appeared in the night sky.

> September 17th. The horizon has grown darker, the air has become fresher, the wind has changed and blows from the north-east, the water is ebbing and some vessels here and there have gone aground. Driving rain follows, lasting all night long.
>
> 22nd. A comet above the horizon in the south-west at the distance of several degrees, its tail is at the top.

23rd. The quarantine, as it seems, is useless here, the more so as there is also one in Kerch where the ships have to stay for a week.

24th. The feud about fishing for sturgeon and beluga is strong between the local people and the Illyrians, Yaninians and Donets Kirgizest.

25th. The export of grain is quite considerable here, but the way they load ships using carts (charettes) which go into the water, often as far as a whole verst, could be improved by using several steamboats with rafts; steamboats are also required in order to go up and down to Kerch which should be regarded as an advanced port before Taganrog, where the traders will, in the course of time, have bread shops for buyers who can come at any season, because the Bosphorus near Kerch knows no winter that could prevent ships from coming or leaving; equally the Don will also be in need of steamboats.

29th. The grapes are very good here, but they cannot make proper wine from them; the grapes are very cheap. Every year they ship 200,000 buckets of grape juice to be made into Champagne. Caiffa, the harbour in Feodosia, will never be important except for shipping products from the Crimea.

Elizabeth had never been so happy, and to Alexander's delight, her health visibly improved. Even the fact that delicacies were hard to come by in such a remote area did little to worry either of them. Relying on local provisions they ate barley soup, fish and lemon jelly nearly every day. Together they spent four peaceful weeks in the mild late-autumn days.

As for Alexander himself, for a time at least, he was as happy as the proverbial sand boy. Mr Hare, whom Lee described as 'a most respectable merchant' in Taganrog, told him that during his visit there, 'he slept upon a straw palliasse, with a small hard pillow of leather'.

The Emperor rose early and breakfasted upon green tea and a small bit of bread. He then walked out and noticed all that came his way. He was frequently up to his knees in mud . . . and took great pleasure in superintending the workmen who were employed in making the public garden, which he had ordered to be formed here. He dined at 2 p.m. and did not appear again on foot, but sometimes afterwards with the Empress in a droshky . . . At the public ball given, he danced with several of the ladies, and remained at least an hour and a half looking at the dances. He was fond of the Polonaise and Scotch dances, and requested that they should be exhibited before him.[83]

Elizabeth was blissfully happy. Nothing in her life had ever equalled the happiness of that time in the little town by the sea. But, as she probably knew in her heart, the idyll was too good to last. Alexander grew restless. He wanted to see the Crimea, the southern part of his enormous empire, hitherto always mysterious, heard of only in travellers' tales until this chance to explore it had suddenly come his way.

CHAPTER THIRTY-ONE

The Fateful Journey

'As soon as the Emperor got into the carriage to depart for the Crimea, the sun appeared on the horizon again', wrote Wylie on 20 September 1825.

> 21st September. The weather is fine, the roads have become better . . . a lot of bustards at the first station.
>
> 25th. We are in Perekop. The distance between the Sivash (Rotten Sea) and the lagoon is from 8 to 9 versts.
>
> 3rd October. The day is cold and dry. The quails are ready to fly away.

Doctor Lee, meanwhile, having visited all the most interesting places in the Crimea, returned from Sevastopol to Odessa on Admiral Greig's yacht. Count Pahlen nearly died of fever on the voyage and Lee wrote that nearly everyone he knew at that time suffered from some form of malaria that year. He himself, having survived a slight attack, reached Odessa on 1 October, just as his employer, Count Vorontsov, set off to meet the Emperor Alexander.

Lee had been back in Odessa for a fortnight when, on 14 October, a letter came from his employer, Count Vorontsov, by then at Taganrog, telling him of the emperor's determination to visit the Crimea and asking him to meet him at Breslau on the Dnieper. Lee set off immediately. 'It was a clear, beautiful night, the road was excellent', and he reached Breslau the following morning at seven o'clock.

In the town, typical of those in the south of Russia, where the shops and bazaars were full of every kind of merchandise, they saw great numbers of wagons laden with salt from the Crimea being dragged through the streets. The country around had been ravaged by the locusts, so that, with little enough for the local people, there was

148

virtually nothing left for the large bodies of troops marching to join the army on the Turkish frontiers.

Leaving Breslau, Lee, with Count Vorontsov, travelled on over an extensive plain of sand to the Perekop Isthmus, the strip of land connecting the vast area of Russia to the small entity of the Crimea. Heading south they reached Simferopol, capital of the Crimea, an ancient Scythian city, but Russian since captured by Catherine the Great in 1784. There they stayed for two nights with Count Fyodor Rostopchin, the general and statesman appointed by Tsar Alexander as governor-general of Moscow, who, accused of responsibility for the fire which had devastated the city on the entry of Napoleon in 1812, had been exiled to the Crimea. A famous breeder of horses based on the Arab and English thoroughbreds, now known as the Russian Saddle Horse or the Russian Riding Horse of the USA, he was at that time mostly concerned with the health of his daughter whom Lee, to his great satisfaction, had treated successfully.

On reaching Yoursouff, Lee's medical skill was again required. This time it was the principal Tartar of the village who had been suffering from intermittent fever, or malaria, for several weeks. Lee gave him calomel and sulphate of quinine, remedies hitherto unknown in the Crimea, which proved so instantly effective that the Tartars believed them to come from a supernatural source.

Driving along the Sea of Azov, Alexander reached the Perekop Isthmus. In the town of Perekop he stayed in the Tartar cottage which Doctor Lee had seen being prepared. Two days later he set out on horseback, riding south over the same unfinished road so recently travelled by Lee, to Simferopol, a distance of about twenty-five miles.

The weather was still warm and the beauty of this newly discovered part of his kingdom was something he could scarcely believe. A few leaves had fallen but most of the trees, particularly the walnuts and figs, were still as green as in summer. Against them, vivid in contrast, were the crimson leaves of wild Russian vines, entwining through branches, climbing to the tops of even the highest trees.

The Emperor arrived at Simferopol on 25 October. Next morning he went to the service in the cathedral before reaching Yoursouff at about four o'clock in the afternoon. With him were General Diebitsch, Sir James Wylie and a few attendants. Lee, in attendance on

Count Vorontsov, was part of the reception party waiting to greet the royal guest. Describing the event in his journal he wrote how:

> When he dismounted from his horse in front of the house at Yoursouff, Count Vorontsov, his aide-de-camp, secretaries and myself, were standing in line to receive him. Though apparently active, and in the prime and vigour of life, the Emperor stooped a little in walking, and seemed rather inclined to corpulence. He was dressed in a blue military surtout, with epaulettes, and had nothing to distinguish him from an army general officer. He shook Count Vorontsov by the hand, and afterwards warmly saluted him, first on one cheek and then on the other. He afterwards shook hands with all of us, and then enquired of me particularly about the health of the Count's children at Biała Cerkiew, whom I had seen not long before. He then enquired if I had visited the south coast of the Crimea during the autumn, and if so, how was I pleased with it. Looking up to the mountains above Yoursouff, and then to the calm sea, upon which the sun was shining, His Majesty exclaimed, 'Was there ever such magnificent scenery!'[84]

Alexander, like so many others, had fallen beneath the spell of this country, so beautiful, so seductive, yet dangerous as the sirens luring sailors to their doom. Little did he or either of his attendant doctors recognize that within this captivating country lay the source of a deadly disease. 'The noxious odours' which rose from swamps and were believed to be the source of infection were certainly unpleasant, but no one at that time realized that the anopheles mosquitoes breeding in the damp ground were actually the carriers of the malaria which, in that late warm autumn, was claiming so many lives.

Lee set off, in advance of Alexander, to ride along the coast to Alupka. All along the road he found Tartars, magnificent, dark-skinned men who had come from all parts of the Crimea to see the emperor pass by. The emperor acknowledged them, enchanted by all that he saw, riding slowly along the coast to the botanical gardens at Nikita, founded some twelve years before.

Later the tsar visited Princess Anna Golitsyn, who lived nearby.

Staying with her were Julie von Krüdner's daughter and son-in-law and some of their religious friends, all of whom, so General Diebitsch noticed, were suffering from what he called 'the ague' – most probably malarial fever.

Alexander then stayed the night with Count Vorontsov, whose estate at Alupka was a short way along the coast from Oreinda. His house, the summer residence of the Governor of Odessa, was at that time one of the most luxurious villas on the south coast of the Crimea, so favoured by Alexander's courtiers in preference to the humbler house at Taganrog.[85]

The same evening, as the count himself, his doctor Robert Lee and James Wylie dined with the honoured guest, the conversation was carried on in a mixture of French and English.

It was noticed that Alexander ate very little. He had stopped, so he explained, to eat fruit along the road. Then as oysters were served it was seen that a small worm clung to one placed before him on his plate. Wylie, however, assured him that it was quite harmless.

He then reminded the emperor of an incident at the conference of Verona, when someone from Venice had sent a message imploring him not to eat oysters as there was a poisonous marine worm or insect inside them. This led to a discussion on the insects of the Crimea and the Ukraine, of which Lee had made a large collection. Alexander asked him if there were any scorpions, scolopendras and tarantulas in the Crimea, to which Lee replied that there were in fact large scorpions. Scolopendras, of great length, he had seen in Odessa but there were none in the Crimea, nor were there any tarantulas. The tsar then talked about the dance which was supposed to cure the bite of the tarantula whereupon Wylie humorously reminded him of how, after a scorpion had been found in his bed in Verona, he had written a prescription for the cure of the bite of the Carbonari!

Then followed a long discussion on homeopathy. Wylie said that he favoured the views of the physicist Samuel Hahnemann, then much in vogue both in Germany and in Russia. He believed that his method of administering extremely small doses of medicines was just as effective as large ones if the patients were kept on a strict diet. Count Vorontsov, anxious to know if this would apply to the fevers of the Crimea, turned to Lee who answered emphatically, and as it proved prophetically, 'that large doses of quinine almost instantly cured these fevers, when small doses proved ineffectual'.

Suddenly, without any warning, Alexander caused a sensation. Turning to the count he thanked him 'for the acquisition he had that day made for him'. It then transpired that, through the agency of Vorontsov, he had just bought the nearby estate of Orianda a few miles south-west of Yalta. Excited as a boy with a new toy he told those around the table of his plans for having a palace built as soon as it was possible. His listeners, enthralled, could barely comprehend the details involved before, to their amazement, in a sudden rush of words, he poured out what was uppermost in his mind. 'When I give in my demission, I will return and fix myself at Orianda, and wear the costume of the Tauria.'

This extraordinary statement brought silence to the table. Doctor Lee, for one, thought he had misunderstood what the emperor had said. However, a short time afterwards, when Count Vorontsov suggested that the large flat open space of ground to the west of Orianda should be made into pleasure grounds for His Majesty, Alexander replied, 'I wish this to be purchased for General Diebitsch, as it is right that the chief of my état-major and I should be neighbours.'

Diebitsch himself was delighted by this news. A somewhat grotesque figure, with his large head and untidy locks of red hair, he was, nonetheless, one of the tsar's truest supporters. Alexander now acknowledged his wish to see him installed in an estate immediately adjacent to the one which he himself proposed to acquire.

From the words that he spoke that night, the general and the rest of the dinner guests gathered that Alexander hoped in the near future either to abdicate in favour of one of his brothers, or to delegate enough of his responsibility as emperor to allow him to live happily, at least in partial retirement, with Elizabeth on the Crimean coast.

This proved the reason for glasses to be filled with the famous Crimean champagne, made from local grapes. Count Vorontsov, rising to his feet, turned to the emperor and asked, 'Sire, may we be permitted to drink the health of Her Majesty the Empress?'

'Most certainly,' replied Alexander, whereupon all of those present rose to join in the toast.

According to Lee's diary, the tsar then thanked Count Vorontsov 'for the excellent entertainment he had provided; and addressing himself to us all, said with kindness and condescension, "Your presence on this occasion has afforded me the greatest satisfaction." '

Walking out of the dining room he climbed some steps up to the flat roof of the house. A small party of Tartars waited to meet him and, looking at them through his eye-glass (he was known to be short-sighted) he exclaimed, 'What handsome oriental countenances! What a fine race of men! One of the most striking peculiarities of the Crimea would be lost if the Tartars were expelled. I hope they will be encouraged to continue here.'

An effendi, introduced to him, presented a petition, 'which he did by bending down and raising his hands to his head, without removing his turban'.

Alexander then went to bed but hardly was he asleep before, in the middle of the night, the thunder of hoofs on the hard ground outside the house woke those within. Alexander got up quickly to meet the courier who had arrived with very disturbing news. A new conspiracy to raise rebellion had been discovered. Later it was to transpire, as Lee recorded, that word had come from an agent named Maybor-odka, revealing that a man called Pavel Ivanovich Pestel, small and sinister as another Napoleon, was behind a cartel of four colonels who were planning to cause a rebellion. The slaves were to be freed immediately; the royal family slain.

General Diebitsch, hastily throwing off the nightcap which covered his sprouting red locks, was summoned twice during the night, from the nearby house in which he was staying, to discuss with Alexander the action that should be taken to suppress the threatened revolt. Certainly Pestel's arrest was ordered, it seems on that very night.

The news was not only disturbing but hurtful to Alexander, who had shown much kindness to the young Pestel, son of the former governor-general of Siberia, for whose education in Dresden he had paid. Returning to Russia at the age of sixteen, Pavel had joined the Corps of Pages in St Petersburg, where he had studied political science. He had then joined the army where fellow officers, who had served in Paris and western Europe, inspired him with ideas of revolution. Transferred to southern Russia, he had organized a local branch of the Society of Welfare where ideas of republican govern-ment and the ways by which the imperial family could be forced to abdicate or to accept the new regime had been the main object of discussion.

Distressed as he was by this treachery of a young man he had done so much to help, Alexander spent a sleepless night. Next morning, however, he gave no outward sign of anxiety, or even of exhaustion, as he rose at his usual early hour.

Summoning Robert Lee, he asked him to walk round the lower part of the garden at Alupka where they could talk in private. Firstly, having described the illness of his wife, the empress, Alexander then asked Lee if he would visit her in a professional capacity at Taganrog. Lee having replied that he would of course be delighted to do so, Alexander then threw back his head and, gazing at the clear sky above him, asked the doctor if he had ever known such beautiful scenery as that of the Crimea. Fired with enthusiasm, he said how much he had enjoyed his visit and how greatly he hoped that the country would soon be full of rich vineyards and flourishing villages and towns.

Lee, in reply, carefully choosing his words, 'hinted, in the most delicate manner that I could, that the frequent occurrence of violent fevers to those who visited the Crimea and to its constant inhabitants, was the only circumstance which appeared to me likely to prevent His Majesty's anticipations being completely realized'.

Alexander then ended the conversation by urging Lee to remain in Russia, attached to Count Vorontsov, the value of whose public services he had now fully realized.

The evening of the previous night's dinner party was long to be remembered by those present. Such was the tsar's happiness that it appeared the troubles which had so long tormented him, particularly his long-held guilt over his involvement in his father's death, had at last been driven from his mind. To all those who saw him on that early November night, Alexander seemed like a man from whom a burden of remorse had been lifted by a decision to transform his life.

The next day, however, due it would seem to a message delivered by the courier, his contentment seemed to vanish. At midday, having shaken hands with Count Vorontsov and all his attendants, to whom he said a fond farewell, he mounted his horse to begin the ride of thirty-something miles to Balaclava.

Lee was among the group who watched with some sadness as the tall, fair-haired figure of the man who had so charmed them all rode at the head of his party out of sight. Little could any of them guess, seeing him sit so easily astride a rather fractious horse, that the seeds of the illness of which Lee, only that morning, had so prophetically warned, were already wasting his strength.

Alexander left the south coast of the Crimea on a late autumn day, which, although beautiful in the morning, would later turn to rain. Clouds darkened the horizon but the sun still shone as the road climbed up through beech woods, shining glorious in the low rays of the sun.

Reaching the foot of the Merdveen the party drew to a halt as it was discussed whether to try to take the shortest route, which meant climbing the mountains before them, to the height of nearly 4,000 feet, and crossing the narrow pass before coming down into the Baidar Valley on the opposite side. Alternatively they could have gone along the coast, through the little town of Foros, an easier but longer route.

Alexander, needless to say, seized the challenge to cross the mountains, looming dark with approaching rain. They had in fact crossed the pass, and were riding downhill into the Baidar Valley when suddenly the weather changed. Thick mist, swirling down from the hilltops, shut out the sun. An east wind blew hard against them and soon it began to rain.

Wearing only a light coat, Alexander became wet, cold and irritable. His temper became worse as his horse continued to mis-behave, shying and stumbling on the badly made road. So dangerous was it that the animal Wylie was riding actually came down, nearly breaking the doctor's leg in the fall.

On reaching Baidar, Alexander dismounted, tired and hungry, to find there was no food on hand. His mâitre d'hôtel had gone on to Sevastopol. Wearily he climbed into an open *caleche*, his horse being led behind. Yet despite his obvious tiredness, when two miles from Balaclava, he mounted again, and rode accompanied by General

Diebitsch to inspect a battalion of soldiers recruited from Greek families in the Crimea. There at last he was able to eat some fish. But his day was not yet done. Alone in the deepening dusk, he rode for at least ten versts[86] to the monastery of St George.

By now it was very cold, a sudden frost setting in. With neither a cloak nor a coat, Alexander stayed for two hours before driving on to Sevastopol, where, having visited the church by the light of flaming torches, and inspected soldiers lining the street, he was too tired to eat anything and instead went early to bed. Wylie, who had gone on ahead to Sevastopol, was much concerned, noting in his diary, 'The Emperor is slightly unwell. One ounce du v-b-re. The news from the Empress was good for him.'

Next morning, however, despite the tsar's now obvious indisposition, the tour continued. He inspected forts, a hospital, a dockyard and ships of the Black Sea Fleet. But as he was driven to Bakhchisarai to meet the Tartar chiefs, he was so utterly exhausted that he slept in the carriage most of the way. Nothing, however, would deter him from completing his pre-arranged itinerary. Riding four miles to the Jewish city of Chufut-Kale, he visited the principal synagogue. Then on he went to a Greek Orthodox monastery, where, climbing some steep stairs, he stumbled, and was forced to stop for a rest, admitting that he felt both giddy and weak. Nevertheless, that same afternoon, he visited several mosques.

At last, he sent for Wylie, under the pretence of asking for news of Elizabeth. But his doctor, noticing his pallor and breathlessness, was not deceived. Questioning Alexander, he eventually got him to admit that he was not feeling well and could not sleep. He then suggested several remedies but was met with a sharp rebuff. 'I know how to treat myself,' Alexander said defiantly and Wylie, aware of the strength of his obstinacy, bowed and quickly withdrew.

The punishing programme continued for another six days through the steppes of the north-western Crimea. Alexander managed to complete his commitments although obviously a sick man., The area was at least fairly flat, although, as Wylie noted in his diary, stretches of foul-smelling marshland were badly infested with mosquitoes. They spent one night at Perekop and the next between the isthmus and Oriekoff.

'Nov 1st. Lake sediments on the left, a house in ruins, another lake on the right, stinky, neither fresh nor salt.'

Then, proving how Alexander, despite his now obvious illness, insisted on punishing himself by travelling long distances and visiting churches and hospitals on the way, Wylie continues to describe his progress in the valley of the Dnieper.

> 2nd. We did 182 versts today to travel to a priest in Znamenka. The hospital in Naslierobomy(?) is in good condition. Bulikovski (?) is good on the banks of the Dnieper: the country is fertile. There is a nobleman here who has 70 thousand sheep . . . The Artillery Hospital in Znamenka is very well maintained.

On the afternoon of the fifth day, in his carriage beside Diebitsch, Alexander was seized with such violent shivering that the general, to his great alarm, heard the tsar's teeth chattering in his head.

That night he drank some hot punch but could not bear the sight of food. Next day it was suggested that he should stop in the town of Mariupol, but Alexander would have none of it. Notwithstanding that he was now obviously very ill, he insisted on returning to Taganrog, a journey of some sixty miles. A closed carriage was found and, wrapped in a bear skin and a great coat, the emperor slept fitfully as, with stops necessitated only by changing horses, he reached the Sea of Azov and the harbour town.

CHAPTER THIRTY-TWO

'Come on, my dear friend. I hope you are not angry with me.'

Elizabeth was horrified as she saw Alexander staggering with exhaustion from the coach on his return to Taganrog. His skin was yellow and he complained that he was deaf. Still he refused to take any of the medicines prescribed by Wylie, except for a little calomel. Neither would he allow himself to be bled. He said that all he wanted were sleep, quiet and cold water, the last of which Wylie did not advise.

Wylie, by now very worried, dating his diary 5th November, described their arrival at Taganrog:

> The night was nasty. Refusal to take medicines. It desolates me. I am frightened that such obduracy may have some bad effects one day.
>
> 6th. The Emperor dined with Her Majesty the Empress and left the table. Fedorov [Alexander's valet] called me from the table to advise me that His Majesty had a perspiration which happened involuntarily – so strong is his aversion to medicine. After a struggle he consented, between 5 and 6 o'clock, to take a dose of pills.
>
> 7th. This fever has a similarity with the endemic Crimean disease. The exacerbations repeat too often for me to assume that it is *Hemitritaeus Semitertiana*, although that extreme weakness, that apathy, those swoons are closely related to it.
>
> 8th. The fever is apparently *Febris gastrica biliosa*; that putrescent eructation, that inflammation on the liver side, despress-corde, vomiting *sine vomitu nec dolore fortiter comprimendo*,

require that premières voies [bowels] be cleared properly. One has to traire [draw] the liver I told Stoffregen [the Empress's doctor].

9th. The Emperor is a little better today, but he is expecting a full recovery from his illness with a perfect belief in God. The condition of the *viscera chylopoetica* may at present indicate to the diarrhoea which was so inappropriately stopped at Bakhchisarai.

10th. Starting from the 8th [day] I have noticed that something occupies his thoughts more than his recovery and troubles his soul *post hoc ergo propter hoc*. He is worse today, and Müller, according to his words, is the cause of it. Prince Volkonsky [the tsar's personal secretary] was, for that reason, instructed to rebuke poor Müller.

Growing weaker and tormented with thirst, Alexander agreed to take a cordial drink, which had been specially prepared. One of his valets tasted it and said it was bitter and Elizabeth did the same. Wylie, however, tried it and said that there was nothing wrong. The drink was almost certainly harmless – nitrous acid, then widely used for fevers, probably giving it a bitter taste. Nonetheless, as was almost inevitable, rumours that the tsar had been poisoned were soon to be on many tongues.

11th. The illness continues; the intestines are quite unclear, *ructus, inflatio*. When I talk to him about blood-letting and laxatives, he gets into a rage and does not deign to talk to me. Today we, Stoffregen and I, discussed the matter. Despite his irritation the Tsar did eventually allow a few leeches to be put to his head.

12th. As far as I remember, tonight I prescribed medicines for tomorrow morning, if we manage, by guile, to persuade him to take them. It is cruel. There is no human power that could bring this man to reason. I am miserable.

13th. Everything will go badly because he will not allow, will not hear, what is indispensable. Such a turn is a very ill omen. His pulse is very irregular, weak and there will be exudation unless one administers *des mercuriaux* (mercurial remedies), *saigne* (blood-letting), patching, mustard, diuretics and purgatives.

14th. Everything is very bad although he is not delirious. I intended to give him *acide muriatique* with a drink but encountered the usual refusal. 'Go away'. I started crying and he, seeing it, said, 'Come on, my dear friend. I hope you are not angry with me for that? I have my own reasons.' ('Venez, mon cher ami. J'espère que vous ne m'en voulez pas pour cela. J'ai mes raisons.')

At times Alexander was delirious, rambling on about the awful carnage of the battles and of the burning of Moscow which plainly obsessed his mind. Then suddenly, fixing his eyes on Wylie, he told him of the death of his father, the crime which had eaten like cancer into his subconscious thought. 'It was a horrible act,' he said to the doctor, who through the years had grown to be his close friend, and who now stood, helpless to save him, by his side. It was clear that the end was approaching and, at Wylie's suggestion, a priest was called in to administer the last rites.

15th. Today and yesterday, what a sad duty was it for me to inform him about his coming destruction, in the presence of Her Majesty the Empress who was going to offer him an efficacious medicine, communion administered by Fedorov.

16th. It all seems too late to me. Only because of the physical and mental exhaustion and diminution of sensitivity did I manage to give him some medicines after the Holy Communion and the parting words by Fedorov.

17th. From bad to worse. See the case history. The Prince [Volkonsky] for the first time took possession of my bed to be closer to the Emperor. Baron Dibisch [*sic*] is downstairs.

18th. Not the slightest hope to save my adored sovereign. I warned the Empress and the princes, Volkonsky and Diebitsch. The former was in his room, the latter was downstairs with the valets.

19th. Her Majesty the Empress, who had spent many hours in my company, stayed alone at the Emperor's bedside all these days until death came at 10 minutes to 11 this morning.

'Come on, my dear friend.'

For two days Elizabeth had sat beside her husband or knelt by the bedside holding or stroking his hand. Her eyes were fixed upon him as he became weaker and weaker until all signs of life were gone. Rising, she closed his eyes, folded his arms over his breast, kissed his hand, and then knelt down by the side of the dead body for half an hour in prayer.

CHAPTER THIRTY-THREE

The Death Certificate of Doubt

Alexander died on 19 November (or 1 December according to Gregorian calendar) 1825. His body was examined by no fewer than ten doctors but it was left to Wylie, deeply grieving for the man who had been not only his patient but his friend, to carry out the autopsy and to arrange for the corpse to be embalmed. It was Wylie who signed the death certificate, giving Crimean Fever as the cause. And in view of the record of his diary there is little or no reason to doubt his word.

> 20th. As soon as His Majesty passed away, even before that, some persons checked his effects and within a short time the papers were sealed; we exchanged our remarks about the envy and sadness for the one who had departed from us.
>
> 22nd. Autopsy and embalming, which confirms everything I foretold. Oh, if only I had had his consent, if he had been compliant and obedient, that surgery would not have taken place here.
>
> 23rd. The complaints by physicians about those in charge of logistics were very justified.

According to one visitor of 1890 the room in which Alexander died was converted into a private chapel. 'Under the altar, in the basement, there is a monument made of rough stone . . . There is a bronze plaque embedded in the monument, which depicts Alexander's death . . . The story goes that Alexander's intestines are buried under that monument.'[87]

The first Robert Lee, at Odessa, knew of what had happened was on the morning of 20 November when Count Vorontsov summoned him into his library. Entering the room he was told by the count that there was bad news from Taganrog – that the emperor was dangerously ill –and that he must hastily pack his bags and set out with him in two hours, to give what assistance he could to the other overwrought physicians who were trying to save his life.

Setting off at noon, the count's carriage rumbled its way across the deep sands by the seashore. The count told Lee that he believed all hope for the emperor was lost. Reaching Nikolaev at midnight, they found Admiral Greig, who, also ignorant of the extent of the emperor's illness, begged Lee to write to him from Taganrog to tell him what was happening there.

Travelling on they found the country so devastated by locusts that the peasants were actually hauling straw from the roofs of their houses to feed cattle that would otherwise starve. Next day, reaching Breslau, they crossed the Dnieper on a raft which had replaced the floating bridge. It was only on the following day, on reaching Taganrog in the evening and being taken by the governor of the town to the house of a merchant, that they learned the sad news. Alexander had died the day before Count Vorontsov had received the letter reporting his illness.

Count Vorontsov, greatly distressed and hardly able to believe that the man whom he had entertained at his house on that memorable evening less than a month before, had died so suddenly, sent his own doctor to Wylie to find out what had occurred.

Sir James read Doctor Lee the whole of his report from the diary so neatly written in his small meticulous hand. His reports had been signed by the other doctors, Stoffregen and the empress's surgeon among them, to whom Wylie, in desperation, had turned to for advice.

In his journal, Lee testifies that, as far as he knew, there was no cause for misgiving concerning Alexander's death.

During the six weeks I remained in Taganrog after the Emperor's death, I never heard that anyone entertained a doubt, or expressed a suspicion, that His Majesty's death was attributable to any other than a natural cause. The physicians who had the care of His Majesty were accused by some, without the slightest ground, of mismanaging the case; and I heard the question repeatedly put: 'Why did they not compel His Majesty to submit to their plan of treatment?' Or, in other words, as Sir James Wylie expressed it, why did they not commit the crime of lèse Majesté – a proceeding which no circumstances could ever justify.

I enjoyed the best opportunities in the Crimea of observing the devoted attachment of Sir James Wylie to the Emperor Alexander, whom he had accompanied in all his campaigns; and I conscientiously believe that on this trying occasion Sir James Wylie discharged his arduous professional duty in a manner worthy of his high reputation.

Wylie's own diary continues to describe the details of Alexander's lying in state: of how he himself placed his body in a coffin, and of his great sadness in being forbidden to accompany the cortège on the long trip from Taganrog back to St Petersburg for burial.

December 3rd. All the documents with the case history sent off today to Dr Klinle for the Dowager Empress by express mail and four days before the departure of Prince Gagarin.

11th. The body taken to the cathedral of the Greek monastery where I was present.

12th. Grand service at the monastery which I attended with sadness.

13th. The prince hinted today that I could leave. However, I need an order from Baron Dibitsch [*sic*] to accomplish it. Read arrives from Petersburg.

14th. I visited Her Majesty the Empress several times. The birthday [Tsar Alexander's][88] the day before yesterday, which I spent in her presence, was the most moving and sorrowful day for me. The Tsarina deserves to be pitied for thousands and thousands of times; no other wish but to die.

17th. I came to have a meal and to see the Volkonsky princesses and the three adjutants. I wrote today to Doctor Klinle sending him the last instructions on preservation.

18th. Within a few days the winter settled in and the sea froze so much as to enable crossing on sledges.

25th. I was busy the whole evening from 7 till 10.30 packing

His Majesty's body. Good God, what a coffin, suitable for nothing; they started to make a new coffin in the cathedral again. I am afraid that the lead may crush the head; everything is made hugger-mugger. But the four adjutants, the generals, Sazonov, the prince and princesses have made sure everything is safe so far.

28th. Today I am going to the Empress to receive her last orders.

29th. I saw my adored sovereign for the last time on earth. Due to the hatred for me, I am deprived of the permission to accompany him all the way through.

The question is, was Alexander really in that coffin – described by Wylie as both makeshift and barely long enough for his height – that was buried eventually in St Petersburg?

The fact that when it was opened on two later occasions, it was found to be empty, gave rise to the legend that Alexander had colluded with Wylie to sign a false declaration (as he had done in the case of his father's death) and, having substituted a body, allowed him to escape to the freedom of anonymity for which he yearned.

The author of an article in a Cologne newspaper in 1933 claimed that Wylie's 'Memoirs', lately found among the Imperial Secret Archives, provided documentary evidence of Alexander's survival. They showed, he wrote, that the body of a courier, killed in an accident a few days earlier, was embalmed, while the tsar, by arrangement with Wylie, boarded an English ship at Taganrog on the night of 18/19 November 1825. In 1841, the article continues, Nicholas asked Wylie, sworn to secrecy, to write a single copy of his 'Memoirs' of the happenings. Each tsar, as was clear from the notes and signatures on the manuscript, undertook to reveal the true course of events to his successor when he came of age. The signatures, according to the writer of this article, were those of Tsar Nicholas II and his brother, Grand Duke Michael.[89]

The author of the article does not reveal how he came about the sources of his claims. However, doubtful as these may be, it does seem certain that Alexander's face was soon unrecognizable even to those who knew him well. The embalmers at Taganrog were amateurs at their trade. His body began to decompose before it even left the town. Elizabeth ordered that his face be covered as he lay for three weeks within the room where he had died. The head was exposed, however, when the body was eventually moved to the church of the Greek Monastery in the town, but by that time the face was black and so disfigured that people shrank back at the sight. Doctor Lee records in his memoirs:

11th December, 1825, Friday. This morning at nine o'clock the body of the Emperor Alexander was conveyed from the house in which he resided to the church called St Alexander Nevsky, which has been fitted up for its reception. The streets were lined with troops. At half past nine the procession set out. A small party of gendarmes commanded by the Master of Police, under his direction, led the way. Then followed the valets, cook, and others employed about His Majesty. Next, the persons employed about the quarantine and others of the town. Then came a number of priests with flags, torches, and crosses, usually carried by funeral processions. Then came a band of singers. After these a number of generals bearing the orders, crosses, etc, of His Majesty. The car was drawn by six horses covered with black cloth. The coffin was exposed at the head. The feet covered with the same yellow gold cloth which I noticed in the chamber of his house. Over the coffin was a canopy of yellow silk. Attached to the car were a number of cords, which were held by some of the most distinguished officers of His Majesty. After these followed a body of Cossacks with their pikes reversed. The day was bitterly cold . . . The Empress's coach followed the hearse . . . Guns were fired at short intervals from the time the procession set out.

12th. I went to the church of St Alexander Nevsky this morning where the Emperor's body was lying in state. There were two Cossacks with drawn swords at each door of the church. A number of slaves or peasants were looking in but not permitted to enter. There was a platform in the middle of the church covered with black. On this was a small elevation covered in red. Over this was placed the coffin surmounted by a canopy. At the feet, on cushions raised on stools covered with red velvet, were the different orders of His Majesty. This was all that remained of the mighty sovereign who had reigned over forty millions of slaves, and whose empire had extended from China to the Baltic Sea, and from the confines of Persia and Turkey to the Arctic Ocean.

PART TWO

CHAPTER THIRTY-FOUR

The Shadow of Confusion

Alexander's body lay in the church at Taganrog for a full three weeks. Nothing could be done until instructions arrived regarding his funeral from the new tsar. On Alexander's death it had been automatically assumed that in accordance with the rule of primogeniture, his brother the Grand Duke Constantine, second eldest of their father's four sons, would succeed to the Russian throne.

At Taganrog, at last, an order came from St Petersburg commanding the authorities and soldiers in the little town to swear allegiance to the new Emperor of all the Russias, Constantine I. This order was complied with on 22 December. But still there was no message regarding the funeral of his brother, lying in state within the Alexander Nevsky Church.

Then two days later, on Thursday, 24 December, a printed document reached the little town on the Sea of Azov. From it came the extraordinary news that three years earlier, in 1822, the Grand Duke Constantine had written a letter to his brother Alexander, 'stating his desire to waive his title to the succession in case of the Emperor's decease, and requesting that the next in line after him should take his place'.[90]

These written instructions, shown first to the Dowager Empress, Maria Feodorovna, and to Alexander himself, had then been put in a sealed envelope together with a statement from Alexander, declaring Nicholas to be his successor, and given to the Council of the Empire to be opened in case of his decease. It was to be the first act of the Council after Alexander's death.

On this being done, however, the Grand Duke Nicholas and the Council, wishing to give Constantine a chance of revoking this agreement, had caused all the troops and authorities in St Petersburg to swear allegiance to him, and had sent off a messenger to Warsaw to invite Constantine to St Petersburg.

Constantine, whose marriage to Princess Anna of Saxe-Coburg had been annulled in 1819, had then defied the Orthodox Church by making a morganatic marriage with his long-term mistress, the Polish Countess Joanna Grudzinska. Technically this did not affect his claim to the succession, but he did not wish to rule the empire, hence his letter to Alexander formally renouncing his right to succeed him in the event of his death. Now, in response to the message from his younger brother Nicholas, Constantine replied that his decision remained unchanged.

By this time, however, on Alexander's death, the royal guards had already sworn allegiance to Constantine, presuming him to be the heir. When it became known that he had forsworn his inheritance in favour of his brother Nicholas, a group of officers based at St Petersburg, led by Nikita Muraviev, Prince Troubetzkoy and Prince Eugene Obolensky, had formed what they called the Northern Society. They aimed to establish a constitutional monarchy with limited franchise, the abolition of serfdom and equality before the law, and they persuaded some of the regimental leaders not to swear allegiance to Nicholas.

Accordingly, on 14 December, a group of officers commanding about 3,000 men assembled in Senate Square. Abjuring the new emperor, they proclaimed loyalty to Constantine and the constitution. The revolt misfired. First Prince Troubetzkoy lost his nerve and failed to appear. Then, although the rebels quickly appointed Prince Obolensky in his place, other regiments, stationed in or near St Petersburg, failed to join the insurgents for fear of what punishment might ensue.

A period of stalemate ensued until, as Nicholas himself appeared, Count Mikhail Miloradovich, a military hero much beloved of the men, was sent to talk to the rebels. He was still trying to reason with them when a shot rang out, fired by one of the officers, and Miloradovich fell dead.

Furious, Nicholas ordered a cavalry charge. But the horses slipped on the icy cobbles, rendering the charge ineffective. Darkness was descending and the new tsar, in desperation, ordered three cannons, loaded with grapeshot, to open fire. The effect was devastating. The rebels fled. Many tried to reassemble on the frozen water of the Neva where, as the ice broke under gunfire, great numbers of them were drowned.

Nicholas was praised for the prompt action with which he had defeated the insurgents. It was, however, a bad portent for the start of his forthcoming reign.

It was not until 10 January 1826, six weeks after Alexander had died, that the funeral procession finally left Taganrog, to begin the journey of 1,200 miles north to St Petersburg. The weather was now very severe. In Taganrog itself the cold was so intense that dead bodies were being brought from the surrounding steppes for burial in the town. The long funeral procession wound its way slowly over the frozen plains. Everywhere crowds gathered to watch, standing in sad and respectful silence as the great funeral coach, drawn by eight grey horses draped in black with the imperial insignia woven into the cloth, was dragged over the country roads through villages and towns. On 15 February, five weeks after it had begun, the procession at last reached St Petersburg. From there it proceeded to Tsarskoe Selo, where the dead tsar's mother insisted on seeing his corpse.

When warned of its decomposition, she refused to be deterred. 'That is my dear Alexander. Oh, how he has wasted away', was all that she said after a cursory glance. The body, badly mummified, was by then obviously almost unrecognizable to anyone who had known Alexander in life. Nonetheless the words of the dowager empress were remembered, and later construed to signify that she herself was uncertain that the body in the coffin was that of her son.

The funeral took place on 25 March 1826. The coffin was placed beside that of Alexander's father, the murdered Paul I, in the small cathedral in the fortress of St Peter and St Paul. The Duke of Wellington, who was present, representing King George IV, described it as 'a terrible ceremony'. He voiced the opinion of many who, like himself, had known and respected Alexander, both for his personal charisma and for his enlightened, if confused, ideals.

CHAPTER THIRTY-FIVE

The Legend

Alexander's wedding ring, which he had worn for thirty-two years, was placed on an icon beside his grave, supposedly to prove his identity. He was dead. He was buried. But the story did not end there. Many people then believed, and some still think to this day, that the corpse in the coffin was a substitute, smuggled in by Wylie at Taganrog in obedience to the orders of Alexander himself.

The Russian love of mystery certainly enhanced this claim. Also the fact that it was now widely believed that Wylie had falsified the death certificate of Tsar Paul (by claiming he had died of apoplexy when strangulation was the cause) strengthened the speculation that he had done the same in the case of his son. The court gossips were to some extent silenced when Alexander's brother Nicholas, now the tsar, made public demonstration of his faith in the Scottish doctor by appointing him personal physician, the post he had held with Alexander for no fewer than twenty-five years.

The theory that Alexander survived and that another, unidentified, body was put in his coffin in his place rests on the fact that in 1836, eleven years after he died, a holy man – or *starets*, as Russian visionaries were called – appeared in the Siberian town of Krasnoufimsk claiming to be the late tsar.

The man, who was guessed to be in his early sixties (Alexander was forty-eight when he died) was tall and slightly bent, as the late emperor had been before his death His facial features were hard to distinguish, being largely concealed by a thick white beard. He wore the black tunic and trousers of a peasant, but for a man of apparently low social standing, he rode a handsome, obviously well-bred white horse.

It was the horse that first attracted attention when it needed to be shod. The blacksmith, intrigued by its strange and rather sinister-looking rider, asked him where he had come from, as he hammered the iron shoes into shape.

The man made an evasive answer but by this time a few local people had gathered, drawn by curiosity as to the identity of this stranger who rode such a noticeable horse. Some pestered him with questions and, on his refusal to answer, bundled him off to the police station, hoping, it would seem, for a reward.

The police were slightly more successful. The man told them that his name was Feodor Kuzmich, that he owned the horse, and admitted that he had no fixed address. The laws against vagrancy being prohibitive, the police then stripped him and reputedly beat him with a rod made of birch branches. He bore the pain silently, and eventually, frustrated by his silence, but highly suspicious as to who he really was, they banished him still farther into Siberia, to the isolated town of Tomsk.

There he worked in a vodka distillery for nearly five years. He got on well with both the management and his fellow workers, all of whom respected his gentle good manners and lack of pretension to be anything other than the *starets*, or holy man, he claimed to be. Nonetheless a rumour seems to have started that he was not of humble birth, but in fact an aristocrat in hiding from the secret police.

In 1842 Feodor Kuzmich, as he still insisted he was called, was moved to another place of exile at Beloyarsk.[91] There he lived in a hut built for him by a Cossack who befriended him. Soon he became a local celebrity as people, discovering he was knowledgeable about much in the outside world, came to his hut to ask for advice on their problems and for spiritual guidance. Soon he attracted so much attention that the local authorities, apparently afraid of his influence, moved him on elsewhere.

Kuzmich then travelled around Russia for a period of about eleven years. Wherever he went he became involved with the local people, particularly with the children, with whom he appears to have shared a special bond. He captivated them with his stories and is known to have taught them grammar, history, geography and religion. Despite his formidable appearance they seem to have taken to him instantly and often came clutching little bunches of wild flowers.[92] From this it can be taken that, whatever his real identity, Feodor, like Tsar Alexander, was possessed of a captivating charm.

With older people he also discussed religion and described past events in St Petersburg with great clarity. Occasionally he let things slip, as when some workmen, making repairs to his hut, annoyed him by noisy hammering and he shouted out, 'If only you knew who I am you would not dare to aggravate me in this way!'

In October 1858, Kuzmich moved back to the outskirts of Tomsk where a merchant called Khromov offered to build him yet another hut on his property. The *starets* accepted and became friends with the merchant's family, particularly with his young daughter Anna, with whom he had long conversations.

Anna recorded in her diary an incident which greatly puzzled her at the time. The *starets* was living with them while his hut was being built and one evening, as the family were sitting round the dining-room table, Anna was reading aloud from a book that had just been published on the reign of Alexander I. She had just quoted: 'Emperor Alexander turned to Napoleon and said to him . . .' when a furious voice from the next room called out, 'I never said that!' The family looked at each other in amazement, realizing who it was who spoke.

Kuzmich ended his days in the hut built for him by Simeon Khromov. As he grew weaker the merchant asked him who he really was. The reply was, as ever, enigmatic. 'Here lies my secret', he whispered, pointing to his heart.

These were the last words he spoke before, just a few hours later, he died, leaving the mystery of his true identity forever unexplained.

But if Kuzmich really was Tsar Alexander, how was another body placed in the coffin, without anyone – other than Wylie and possibly one or more of the other doctors who attended him – knowing what was taking place?

A picture of him on his deathbed, painted in 1827, shows several black-coated figures standing in the room while Elizabeth sits by his bed. The Russian artist Kulakov, however, two years after Alexander's death, must have relied on hearsay as to the actual number of persons in the room. More factually, the English Doctor Lee, who was present, left a detailed description of the tsar's death. If the legend is true, Lee's account must be an invention and Elizabeth, together with Wylie, must have been party to the deception that then took place.

Certainly the embalmers at Taganrog were inefficient, but if another body, already in a state of decay, was secretly smuggled into the coffin, Alexander's closest attendants, including his wife, must have been involved in a conspiracy to allow him to escape.

It has been suggested that Elizabeth's long sojourn at Taganrog had sinister implications, but the official explanation that her weak heart and well-known infirmity precluded the long journey back to St Petersburg was verified by her death on the way north.

Surmising that Alexander did survive, the next obvious question is how was he spirited, unseen, from the house at Taganrog? Is it indeed possible that, as has been suggested, he was somehow transferred, presumably disguised and under cover of darkness, from the house to Lord Cathcart's private yacht?

William Shaw, 1st Earl Cathcart, as British ambassador to St Petersburg had been with Alexander all through the war with France. Travelling together, in close company, they had become firm friends. It may have been nothing more than coincidence but during Alexander's visit to Taganrog, Cathcart's yacht was seen lying in the harbour flying a British flag. This was quite odd, the little town on the Sea of Azov being far from a fashionable resort. What is more extraordinary, however, is that the yacht raised anchor and left the harbour on the very day that Alexander allegedly died.

Should there be any truth in the theory that the tsar was thus secretly removed by sea, the next question that arises is what happened to him during the eleven years before, as the *starets*, he appeared in Siberia in 1836. One explanation that has been put forward is that he lived as a monk in a monastery somewhere in the Holy Land during those missing years.

Finally the intriguing question remains as to who Feodor Kuzmich really was, if not Tsar Alexander as people finally took him to be?

One possibility, suggested by Grand Duke Nikolai Mikhailovich, is that this man, so obviously well educated and knowledgeable about events at the court of St Petersburg and of incidents in the Romanov family life, was Simeon, the illegitimate son of Tsar Paul and a mistress of his called Sophia Chertorzhskaya.[93]

This would certainly explain the physical resemblance to Alexander, Simeon being his half-brother. Simeon, however, having been educated in St Petersburg, had then gone to England where he had joined the Royal Navy and served on HMS *Vanguard*. Supposedly he died of fever or else was drowned in the Baltic, but neither version is verified and the grand duke failed to find any official record of his death.

Alternatively, it has been suggested that Kuzmich was a man of noble birth, possibly Nikolai Andreyevsky, a cavalry officer, who became a chamberlain in the imperial court. Otherwise several men of similar standing could conceivably have impersonated Alexander among the gullible people of a remote part of Russia.[94]

Feodor Kuzmich died in 1864 by which time, were he really Alexander, he would have been eighty-five. This is another reason why, at a time when the average life expectancy was shorter than that of today, it is unlikely that they were one and the same. Two years later, however, speculation over the tsar's death was further intensified when, on two separate occasions, his tomb was opened and found to be empty inside.

It is feasible that the tsar's body was removed by his nephew, Alexander II, and buried secretly in the graveyard of the Nevsky Monastery in St Petersburg. If so he may have honoured the known wishes of his uncle, who had hated the thought of burial in the fortress of St Peter and St Paul, beside the father he felt he had murdered. Should this have happened Alexander must now lie beside the warrior prince whose exploits, during his lifetime, he had greatly revered.

The enigmatic figure of Sir James Wylie, Tsar Alexander's personal doctor, the one man who knew for certain of the manner of his death, was among those who mourned at his funeral in March 1826. Distinguished by his height, he stood, black-garbed, with bowed head, as the coffin containing the body of the man he had known, served and loved, was placed beside that of his father in the monastery of the Fortress of St Peter and St Paul on that day in March 1826.

What secret was Wylie hiding? For the lack of further evidence no one now will ever know. At the time his sorrow was evident, compounded, so the watchers believed, by his known failure to have forced the tsar to agree to the treatment which may conceivably have saved his life. Secretive as ever, Wylie imparted his knowledge to no one. Turning away from the grave, he left the church a sad and isolated man.

CHAPTER THIRTY-SIX

City of Secret Sedition

It is from Doctor Robert Lee's diary that the impression arises of the state of political tension in Russia following the Decembrist Rising of December 1825. People lived constantly in fear, afraid that even their most private conversations would be overheard and taken as reason for arrest.

Lee also gives vivid descriptions of the country itself at that time. Leaving Taganrog on 10 January 1826 (the day after the funeral procession had set off for St Petersburg), he travelled with Count Vorontsov to Odessa through the worst of the Russian winter. The temperature frequently fell to below 16° Fahrenheit and the wind howled with the full force of a hurricane from Siberia over the vast plains down to the south of the Ukraine.

So intense was the cold that Lee had kept himself occupied in Taganrog by carrying out an anatomical examination of the victims of hypothermia brought in from the steppes to the town. Reaching Odessa he found the general consensus to be that the nation had been saved from revolution by the courage and decision of Emperor Nicholas on the fateful day of 14 December.

Lee was deeply distressed, however, to find that some of the greatest friends he had made during his time in Russia had been proved to be involved in the conspiracy to overthrow the emperor and the government. Foremost among these was General Michael Orloff, a hero of the war against France. Lee had been his guest in his house in Kiev as recently as the previous June. Orloff's wife was both beautiful and intelligent and their household a particularly happy one.

The general, a most perfect host, had taken him on a tour of places of interest, including the catacombs, dug out of the rock, which contained the bodies of more than 100 bishops, saints and historians. However, in private he had confessed to his loathing of the treatment of slaves and of the corrupt state of the government. Nonetheless, absorbed as he was in the study of political economy and sciences, he had given no hint of being in any way involved in a plot to raise a rebellion, let alone to destroy the royal family.

Now charged with treason, this intellectual, civilized man, for whom Lee had such respect and affection, was incarcerated in the dungeon of the fortress in St Petersburg, renowned, as Lee knew, for the dreadful acts of bestial cruelty which took place within its walls.

Another prisoner, the Polish Count Olizar, so recently a guest of Count Vorontsov in the Crimea and known to be in very poor health, was fortunately soon liberated. Not so Prince Serge Volkonsky, who was held without trial, had his sword broken over his head, and, stripped of his rank and honours, was banished to the wilds of Siberia reduced to the rank of a slave.

Due to the unrest in Russia following Alexander's death, Count Vorontsov found it necessary to travel to St Petersburg despite the still freezing weather of the early spring. Together with his doctor he set off from Odessa to begin the long journey from the south to the north on 15 March. Travelling on, at first over the steppes and then through vast areas of forest, they finally reached the capital after nearly four weeks, on 11 April.

Lee, describing how they entered the city about midday, wrote:

I was struck with astonishment at the grandeur of the quays, palaces, public buildings and the bridges of granite over the canals . . . Streets paved, the greatest cleanliness, and crowds of people moving about in every direction. I could not help contrasting this with the miserable villages and people I had left behind in White Russia.

After dinner I went with Colonel A. Rajewsky to take a sail on the Neva. He told me that 250 persons were implicated in the conspiracy . . . We sailed under the Bridge of St Isaac to the Bourse, and from the point on which it stands saw at one view the fortress with all the buildings above it, and on the right the line of palaces and houses upon the quay. The sun was just setting and its rays were beautifully reflected from the broad stream of the Neva, and from the windows of the palaces along its shore.

Soon Colonel Rajewsky was to confide in Lee the details of what had been intended by those involved in the intrigue to overthrow the regime. A constitutional government was to be established along the lines of that in America. The serfs were to be freed; the imperial family destroyed. Lee went with the colonel to visit his sister, the lovely Princess Volkonsky, and found her, as he put it, 'overwhelmed with grief'. She had no idea what would happen to her husband, whether his life would even be spared.

On 28 April, Mr Landers, brother-in-law of the British Consul in Odessa, arrived in St Petersburg. He brought the news that it was now thought to be inevitable that Russia and Turkey would soon be at war once again.

The crisis had been initiated by Tsar Nicholas demanding the ratification of the Treaty of Bucharest, which had been signed by old General Kutuzov and ratified by Alexander on 28 May 1812, the day before Napoleon invaded Russia. The agreement had ended the conflict between the Ottoman and Russian Empires, which had lasted for six years since 1806. Under its terms the Prut River had become the border between the two empires, thus leaving Bessarabia under Russian rule. Russia had also gained the valuable trading rights on the Danube. The Turks, naturally resentful, now wished to reassert their claims.

Troops were being marshalled and the Russian navy under Admiral Greig was preparing for action at sea. Sir James Wylie, head of the army medical department, was ordered to prepare for war. Then suddenly, and surprisingly, the Turkish government, initially so hostile, agreed to the new tsar's terms.

Doctor Lee, who saw Wylie at this moment, claimed he was visibly disappointed. This surprising remark, in view of Wylie's known hatred of the inevitable carnage of war, leads one to believe that, relieved as he must have been that further wide-scale slaughter had been avoided, he was frustrated by the anti-climax of the peace, which had rendered all his preparations useless after weeks of pressurized activity, exhausting to a man of his age.

Lee, in fact, went to the Artillery Hospital and found the wards 'in excellent order'. He was told that the term 'cardiopalmus', invented by Wylie to describe palpitations, was now applied to all the diseases of the heart and great blood vessels 'which I was told are extremely common in the officers and soldiers of the Russian army'.[95]

Wylie had recently published in Russian his *Practical Remarks on the Plague*, which appeared in print at the same time as his translation from the English of James Johnson's influential book on *The Influence of Tropical Climate on European Constitutions*.

On 3 May Lee dined with a wealthy English merchant. Among the guests was a Mrs P (presumably an English woman), who had known Tsar Alexander and been a close friend of Elizabeth's. She told him that the empress had left Taganrog and had managed the first part of the journey tolerably well. There was some anxiety about her health, however, for her feet were swelling and it was feared she had water on the lungs, which appeared to be hereditary as several of her family had died 'of water on the chest'.

Elizabeth had, thankfully, escaped the funeral service and everything that it involved. Too ill to travel with the funeral cortège in January, she had stayed at Taganrog until the snow melted on the steppes to the north. Then she had begun the journey, with her own physician Doctor Stoffregen and her ladies-in-waiting in attendance. Travelling in stages of only fifty miles a day, she was nonetheless exhausted and painfully breathless. On the evening of 15 May she stopped at Belev where, early the next morning, her maid found her dead in bed.

Elizabeth's funeral took place on 14 June 1826. Rumours were circulating that anonymous letters had been sent to Tsar Nicholas, warning him of a probable attempt at assassination. Subsequently, Nicholas and his Etat-Major reviewed the troops at a gallop, saluting each regiment as he passed before the funeral began.

The great concourse of people who came to pay their last respects included many tradespeople, draped in black and carrying black flags, and girls belonging to the different schools which Elizabeth had patronized. Lancers and a long company of priests walked in the procession, which followed the funeral carriage drawn by eight grey horses. At the head, the new emperor and empress and generals and officers preceded a long line of cavalry and horse artillery. There was no music, only the sombre crash of guns fired every minute from the fortress of St Peter and St Paul.

CHAPTER THIRTY-SEVEN

Invasion and Rebellion

Conspicuous among those attending the funeral was a man who stood almost a head taller than most of the surrounding crowd. Although now nearly sixty, Sir James Wylie was still a distinguished figure, his back erect, his hair turning grey. No one present regretted Elizabeth's passing more than he. His thoughts must have rested on the time when, as a young man of thirty, he had first entered the royal household when Elizabeth, the fair-haired princess from Baden, with the beauty of a fragile flower, had been only twenty-four.

How well he remembered his pity for her as he had seen her humiliated by Alexander's parents, dominated by his imperious mother and terrorized by his father's sarcasm and fits of uncontrollable rage. He had witnessed her sadness at the deaths of their two little daughters, one only a baby, the other just a year old. Wylie had watched them both suffer and witnessed, to his sorrow, how Alexander had found solace with his mistress while Elizabeth retired, almost to obscurity. Afterwards, it had seemed miraculously, he had seen Alexander turn to Elizabeth, inspired by her faith in religion, after the disasters of Borodino and the fall of Moscow had sent him almost insane.

As witness to their married life together, Wylie knew, as did few others, that Alexander, unfaithful as he had been, had really loved only Elizabeth, the frail and near ethereal beauty chosen for him by his grandmother when he was only fifteen. He also knew that Elizabeth, admired as she had been by others, including Prince Adam Czartoryski, her husband's friend and confidant, had never loved anyone but Alexander, without whom the world had no pleasure for her. Crowding out times of unhappiness was the image of those halcyon days at Taganrog before the onset of his fatal disease. Alexander's death had clouded her existence. He alone had been her sun.

Doctor Lee describes in his journal how, following the empress's funeral, the city of St Petersburg remained in mourning, the carriages draped with black cloth. He called on Sir James Wylie, who had just received a letter from the empress's personal physician, Doctor Stoffregen, describing his own great sorrow at her death.

He also gave the results of the post mortem, which confirmed Wylie's own diagnosis of the causes relating to her death. Elizabeth's lungs had been found to be sound but her heart was badly diseased. Wylie knew, however, as did Stoffregen himself, that for all her poor physical condition, Elizabeth, without Alexander, had simply not wanted to live.

On the day after Elizabeth's funeral Doctor Lee left St Petersburg. A cold north wind was blowing, setting up clouds of dust. Setting off for Moscow at two o'clock in the afternoon, he was accompanied by General and Madame Naryshkin, she who as Alexander's long-time mistress had caused such grief to his wife. In addition to this strangely assorted party there travelled a Mr Artemieff.

Reaching Tsarskoe Selo after six hours, at eight o'clock, Lee saw for the first time the palace that had been Alexander's childhood home and where he and Elizabeth had spent such a happy time together shortly before leaving for Taganrog in the previous September. His presence could still be sensed, particularly in his rooms, spartan in their simplicity, which were kept just as he had left them.

On a table in each apartment were materials for writing and a small spy-glass. [Alexander, known to have been short-sighted, apparently never wore spectacles.] In his bed-room were his boots, fixed by a hook to his sofa; his two swords, hat, and two pairs of gloves, at the side of a mirror. There was a small table near the side of his bed, on which stood his dressing-case in leather. In a small cabinet adjoining this was his library. Among the books were several on the French Revolution and the Art of War, Sir Walter Scott's novels and *Lalla Rookh*. There were several portraits on the walls: one I believed of Madame Narishkin.[96] The colonnade of Mr Cameron is a work of great beauty. Around it were placed a great variety of statues; but I had not time to examine them. The walks were in the highest order, and there were clumps of trees precisely like those in our English parks. There was an English farm close to the palace, where was a dairy, merinos, &c.

Leaving Tsarskoe Selo the party continued via Novgorod, Torzhok and Tver to Moscow travelling along the new road from the new capital to the old on which 12,000 soldiers were working. A great deal of the country being marshland, they were forced to build causeways which were surfaced with broken granite, a method recently devised by the Scottish pioneer of road construction, John Loudon McAdam.

Until they reached Tver the road was hemmed in with what appeared to be impenetrable forests. They met large herds of oxen being driven towards St Petersburg by men who, in Lee's words, were 'the greatest savages I had ever seen. The state of the agriculture was wretched until we reached Torzhok – the earth was merely scraped. The plough was drawn by one horse, a sort of miserable pony.'

In some places they passed villages belonging to the Crown. Their inhabitants, called Yemshieks, who had more freedom than most peasants, kept the post horses, 1,000 in each place.

In contrast to the countryside Torzhok was a wealthy city thanks to the production of leather used for boots and shoes together with a multitude of other purposes throughout the whole of Russia. Tver was also a large city on the River Volga, its wealth founded on commerce.

Finally the party reached Moscow. Count Vorontsov's house, burnt by the French, was rebuilt, although not yet fully furnished. Lee had another attack of the recurrent Crimean Fever, but once recovered he went to see the Kremlin.

The Kremlin is, I suppose, more than two versts in circumference. It is entirely surrounded by a wall of brick, with little turrets at the top. It encloses a great variety of churches, the Palace of Justice, the Arsenal, the Imperial Palace, and Public Offices of various descriptions. The whole city, with its numberless palaces and churches, was extended out from this ancient residence of the Tsars. Scarcely any marks were left of the conflagration during the French invasion.

General Naryshkin told Lee that when taken prisoner by the French an officer had told him that orders had been given to blow up the Kremlin, and that the report of a cannon would be the signal for the explosions. A very short time afterwards the report of a cannon had been heard, to be followed by three tremendous explosions. The arsenal, totally destroyed, was still being rebuilt when Lee's party arrived.

On the following day Lee went again to the Kremlin, this time with General Naryshkin, to see the preparations for the new tsar's coronation. Within the palace they entered the great hall, built in the Gothic style with a large pillar supporting the roof. The walls were covered with crimson velvet. The throne, in a corner, stood beneath a curtain of purple velvet lined with ermine.

Continuing through the palace, refurbished since French occupation, in the south-west angle they were shown the room occupied by Napoleon, where, from a window with a wonderful view of the city, he had watched Moscow burn.

Next they visited the cathedral, where the walls and even the doors were completely covered with paintings. Sacred among the relics was a nail said to have come from the Holy Cross, and a bit of the Virgin's skirt. Also in the sacristy was the testament of the late Emperor Alexander kept in a box of gold and platinum, under a glass case on top of which was painted a human eye.

Much of the gold and silver in the cathedral had been taken by the French but many of the pictures were still surrounded with emeralds and other precious stones. Cleaning was in progress and such was their veneration that Lee saw people in front of the pictures placing their heads on the ground, then rising and crossing themselves 'with a fervour that was quite astonishing; they went on doing so until exhausted by fatigue'.

It was in this same Cathedral of Assumption, so well described by Robert Lee, that on 3 September, on a brilliantly hot day, the coronation of the new emperor took place.

For James Wylie, attending in his dual official capacity as doctor to the court and director of the medical services, the ceremony must have evoked memories of Alexander's coronation, almost twenty-five years before to the day.

Once again Moscow was *en fête*, guns thundered, bells pealed and crowds cheered in adoration at the sight of their handsome new tsar, but no one knew better than his doctor of the sadness dogging Nicholas's mind

Only twelve days had passed since five leaders of the Decembrists had been hanged. Nicholas had had no option other than to order their death as convicted traitors. Yet all were known to him, Prince Troubetzkoy, in particular, having been a personal friend.

Those spared capital punishment were banished to Siberia, yet, just as the coronation was over, Nicholas ordered that their fetters be released. Many were to spend years in exile, it would appear in a reduced, but nonetheless, comfortable style.

The new tsar returned to St Petersburg, just as his brother had done a quarter of a century before, to find himself faced with a national crisis. Alexander had come back to his capital to confer with King Frederick William over the threat of Napoleon. Now, Nicholas was told that hordes of Persian soldiers had invaded the Caucasus.

And so it was war once more. Three months later the Russian army triumphantly captured Erivan (Yerevan) and by October was threatening the shah's capital of Tehran. On 22 February 1828, the Treaty of Turkmenchay was signed, by which Russia gained the provinces of Erivan and Nakhichevan, together with the exclusive right to keep a fleet of warships in the Caspian Sea.

War then broke out again with Turkey. On 15 March 1828, Nicholas ordered his army to occupy the principalities of the Danube. On 8 June the Russian troops crossed the great river and Nicholas, who had joined his army, found himself being fired at by Turkish guns. He survived unscathed, but the war did not prove to be the easy victory that had been predicted. Terrible epidemics soon ravaged the Russian troops. Devastated by typhus and cholera the army lost fewer men from fighting than from disease. At last the port of Varna, on the coast of the Black Sea, fell to the Russian army. But still the struggle continued, with appalling loss of life.

The campaign of 1829 began quietly, with the Turks still making a stubborn defence. Then at last General Diebitsch, the Silesian who had travelled with Alexander throughout the Crimea, achieved an outstanding victory at Kulevchi on 11 June. On 30 June Diebitsch won another great victory in Silistria and on the same day General Paskévitch, the erratic and ruthless commander who was one of the tsar's most trusted friends, defeated the Turkish army in the Caucasus.

Diebitsch then crossed the Balkans and took Adrianople. It seemed that Constantinople must now fall. The sultan was at his mercy but Nicholas, in consultation with a committee, concluded that it was better to keep Turkey as a country within Europe rather than totally annihilate it as a power. Talking to the Austrian ambassador he said, 'The Ottoman Empire is a state falling into decay . . . but I do not want to overthrow it, I do not need to . . . I only wish for peace.'

Subsequently, on 14 September 1829, the Treaty of Adrianople was signed. By its terms the sea routes of the Bosphorus and the Dardanelles were secured for Russian ships. Turkey ceded fortresses and agreed to pay reparation, and while affirming the rights of the Wallachian principalities, proclaimed Greece a vassal state. Diebitsch and Paskévitch were made Field Marshals and throughout the empire bells rang out in joyful celebration of the victory.

The fact that Sir James Wylie is not named as being present with the emperor on this campaign suggests that, at the age of sixty, he now confined himself to administrative work. Nonetheless, despite increasing age, he is known to have remained as Director of the Russian Military Services until 1838, when, at the age of seventy, he retired.

He was certainly still in office when, on 8 September 1830, the news that a group of dissidents in Poland had risen in rebellion reached St Petersburg. Resentment against the tsar had been gradually increasing as it was felt that the privileges granted by Alexander were being undermined by his brother's autocratic rule. However, it was the report that the Polish army was to join the Russian in suppressing a rising in the Belgian provinces of the Netherlands, aimed to give Belgium independence, which finally set the fuse alight.

Poland had been ruled by the Grand Duke Constantine, appointed by Alexander as governor general of the country of which he himself was king. Constantine, whose second wife was Polish, believed that the army, largely his own creation, was loyal to him, as indeed some regiments proved to be. Nonetheless, on the night of 29 November, a party of revolutionaries broke into his palace, the Belvedere, in Warsaw. They killed the Prefect of Police but Constantine, who was small and snub-nosed like his father, escaped through a secret door, dressed, it is said, in women's clothes.

On 25 December the members of the Polish Diet announced their decision to abolish Nicholas and his descendants as emperors of Poland. Following this the United Chambers of the Diet proceeded to elect a national government under the leadership of Prince Adam Czartoryski, the man of saturnine countenance who, while a great admirer of Elizabeth, had once been Alexander's closest friend.

On 5 February, even as the new constitution was still under discussion, Field Marshal Diebitsch, as he had become, led an army into Poland. On the 19th he reached the walls of Warsaw, but suddenly, and true to the pledges given by his brother that Russia would not attack Poland, came the order from Constantine to cease fire.

However, the fighting continued and the dread disease of cholera once again took its deadly path through the soldiers of both armies. Field Marshal Diebitsch, survivor of so many battles, was among the victims this time, and Grand Duke Constantine also died of the virulent infection, only four hours after the symptoms first appeared.

From Poland the cholera spread north through Russia to reach the capital of St Petersburg. A letter written by his niece reveals that Sir James Wylie, although already fully involved in the endless administration of the medical department of the army, was asked by the emperor to take on the extra responsibility of control of the disease throughout the city.

Somehow, he was successful. The drastic but necessary treatment, involving the rigorous isolation of areas where cholera sufferers were known to be, proved to be effective.

Field Marshal Paskévitch, in command of the Russian army, then led another campaign against Warsaw in August 1831. Overcoming desperate resistance, he entered the capital in triumph on 8 September. 'Warsaw is at the feet of Your Majesty' was the message that Nicholas received.

The fall of Warsaw proved to be the end of the rising, which, as Prince Czartoryski claimed, might well have succeeded had it taken place earlier while the Russian army was embroiled in the Turkish campaign. Nicholas was merciless in his treatment of Poland, the country to which his brother Alexander, following the Treaty of Vienna, had given a statute of independence, with himself proclaimed as king. Then it had been acknowledged as one of the most advanced countries in Europe. Now the Organic Statute of 1832 put Poland once again under Russian dictation at the will and disposition of the tsar. A new prison, built at the gates of Warsaw, symbolized the constitution of an autocrat who ruled with despotic might.

CHAPTER THIRTY-EIGHT

The Winter Palace

Sir James Wylie was no longer a young man. Gone were the days when he and Alexander travelled the length and breadth of Russia at breakneck speed. Nonetheless, despite his more static circumstances, he remained one of the most powerful men in Russia, as contemporary records prove. As Chief Army Medical Inspector, he was also influential in the administration of the medical academies he had founded early in Alexander's reign, in addition to which, together with Alexander Crichton, he became an honorary member of the Russian Imperial Academy of Sciences.

For some time previously the framework his regulations provided for the operation of the Medico-Chirurgical Academy had begun to seem too narrow for him. From the 1820s, a panel under his supervision had been working on a revised version of the Regulations, which was approved in December 1835. It provided for an increase in the faculty, broadening of clinical training and larger funds to maintain the institution. Three years later, on 8 December 1838, Wylie resigned as the president of the academy, which essentially owed its reputation to his service.

Wylie continued to live in his suite of rooms in the Winter Palace until, along with the royal family itself and the rest of the inhabitants, he was forced to move out into temporary accommodation following a disastrous fire.

In 1833 the French architect Auguste de Montferrand was commissioned to redesign the eastern state rooms and create the Field Marshal's Hall and the Small Throne Room. De Montferrand, who had already designed the magnificent St Isaac's Cathedral, the golden dome of which dominates the skyline of St Petersburg today, was also the creator of the Alexander Column in the Palace Square. This single monolith of red granite, over eighty-three feet in height, surmounted by an angel holding a cross – the face said to be modelled on Alexander's – was a tremendous feat of engineering erected to commemorate Alexander's victory over Napoleon in the war with France.

The architect, pressed by Tsar Nicholas to complete the job of modernizing the Winter Palace in a short space of time, in some places had substituted wood for stone. Somehow a fire started and the chimneys of unused fireplaces, covered by newly made wooden partitions, acted as flues for the flames which spread undetected from room to room until the whole building was ablaze. Heroically the palace guards and the servants managed to save many priceless treasures, which were piled up in the snow outside in Palace Square.

Most of the treasures within the Winter Palace were saved but then came new terror as it was realized that the Hermitage, the world-famous museum attached to the palace, was also at risk from the devouring flames. This building, founded by Catherine the Great in 1764, housed Voltaire's library of 6,780 volumes in all, an immense number of histories, and even a collection said to have been made by the empress for her valets to prevent idleness.

More famously, the museum held the unique collection of 225 European paintings by western European artists, including Raphael, Titian, Leonardo da Vinci, Murillo, Rembrandt, Rubens, Van Dyck and Nicolas Poussin among many others. All had been obtained by the empress from the Berlin merchant Gotzkowsky as the foundation of collection, since enhanced by her grandsons, tsars Alexander and Nicholas, who followed her reign.

Now it was the younger of those who, as the Winter Palace burned, avoided what might have been a still greater calamity with great presence of mind. Knowing the value of the irreplaceable works of art in the Hermitage he ordered that the three passages leading from the palace itself to the building be destroyed to create a fire break. By his prompt action he saved what was then, and has continued to be, one of the greatest art collections in the world.

Nonetheless his palace was all but destroyed by the fire. The poet Vasily Zhukovsky called it 'a vast bonfire with flames reaching the sky', which continued to burn for several days.

Even as the palace was smouldering, the tsar ordered it to be rebuilt within a year, with almost unbelievable results. With the temperature still well below freezing, work began and no fewer than 6,000 men were employed. Some died as they laboured, either from accidents, illness, or sheer physical fatigue. Nonetheless others immediately replaced them and the rebuilding was completed within the allotted time.

The structure was strengthened with the latest inventions of the developing industrial age: the roof supported by a metal framework and the ceilings in the great reception rooms with iron girders. Greatest of innovations was the Jasper Room, which, having been totally burned out, was replaced by the even more magnificent Malachite Drawing Room as the principal reception room of the tsarina's suite.

One practice that was discontinued after the ruinous fire was the keeping of cows in the attics under the roof. The animals, needed for fresh milk, nonetheless produced odorous manure and the tsar, who had a keen sense of smell (he forbade smoking in the palace and even in the streets) may have detected it.

The Winter Palace, of which the principal façade measures 500 feet in length, is believed to contain 1,057 rooms, 1,945 windows and 1,786 doors, together with innumerable staircases and passages connecting the many suites of rooms. In Wylie's day, while the ground floor was mostly offices, the royal family lived on the first floor above. The Jordan Staircase, so named because the emperor descended from it at Epiphany, when the waters of the Neva were blessed by priests, led from the state, or ambassador's entrance, up to the great reception rooms, branching off from either side. Redecorated largely in the rococo style, these were the scene of the lavish receptions, which as the Chief Army Medical Inspector, Wylie was commanded to attend.

Possibly, as he grew older, he found these public duties a physical strain. With no chairs provided, everyone was made to stand. The scale of entertainment was enormous. The dining room alone could seat 1,000 while the state rooms, on occasion, were crammed with at least 1,000 more guests. The restored building was well heated with countless fires and stoves. The rooms and corridors were filled with the scent of hothouse plants as outside the temperature fell far below freezing and the river became near solid with ice.

As a trusted friend of the family to which he had been so long attached, Wylie was present at Romanov family weddings, when the bridal procession walked from the Malachite Drawing Room, through the state rooms, to the Palace Grand Church.

Yet for all the palace's magnificence, the tsar himself lived a life of austerity within its walls. Obsessed as he was with his army, Nicholas slept on a camp bed on a mattress filled only with straw.

Wylie himself, according to his great niece, 'usually sat in a small room containing only a writing table and two chairs and half a dozen favourite dogs lying on the floor. When at home he, soldier like, made his midday meal on black bread and salt but frequently, according to the custom of the country, he went to some acquaintance, either in the palace or the city, where he dined as a member of the family.'[97]

Renowned for being careful with money, he was not opposed to gaining some financial return for promoting the tsar's favourite hair oil, Rowland's Macassar Oil. The famous hair tonic, discovered by Tsar Nicholas, one imagines on his visit to London in 1844, had to be sent to Russia by the makers. So dark and pungent was the oil that it gave its name to the antimacassars which began to be spread over the backs of seats in railway carriages throughout Europe and likewise used by house-proud Victorians in Britain to protect their sofas and chairs. The oil was sold in bottles, each one of which, even 100 years later, was wrapped in a leaflet containing a copy of a letter from Sir James Wylie, Physician at the Court of St Petersburg, which ran: 'I have it under command from His Imperial Majesty that you will without delay send ten guineas' worth!'

It was not only hair oil that came from Britain: Wylie's aged but still indomitable mother, Janet, announced she was coming to visit him. He did his best to stop her, but determined as ever, she somehow made the long journey, presumably by sea, to arrive triumphantly in St Petersburg.

Wylie's youngest brother Walter, captain of a ship called the *Baronet* (doubtless in Sir James's honour) visited several times. Landing in St Petersburg, he was summoned to an audience with the tsar. Asked to dine at the palace, he was much impressed by the gold plate but even more so by the courtesy of Tsar Nicholas, who, despite the fact that French was the language usually spoken, insisted on this occasion that those who were present spoke English throughout the evening to avoid embarrassing his guest. Walter also left Russia with presents of a beautiful gold and platinum cup and saucer and two very large and valuable diamond rings. At a later date his son, then a sailor boy, was given a large silver pen and pen holder by his uncle who, if parsimonious in some ways, was certainly indulgent to his relations.

As he grew older, Wylie became renowned for his eccentricities. Nonetheless, such was the affection of the royal family and eventual esteem of the colleagues whose jealousy had so greatly plagued his early years that he came to be regarded in St Petersburg with the reverence due to his age.

It was in 1838, following its restoration, that Wylie left the Winter Palace to live in the house he had bought in the street known as the Galerney, near the English Quay. It was here that the American Doctor Channing was to find him some sixteen years later. Now aged over seventy, Wylie chose to retire from his positions as Chief of the Military Medical Department and President of the Royal Medico-Chirurgical Medical Academy, which he had held for thirty years since 1808. Nonetheless, although eased from some of his responsibilities, as a privy councillor, a rank that no physician in the Russian service had ever reached before, he remained significant in the government of the autocratic tsar. Already having been awarded Russian noble rank, in 1828, he held the Russian orders of St Vladimir, 1st Class, the diamonds of the St Alexander Nevsky order and St Ann order.

Rulers of other countries who had adopted his medical practices also honoured him with decorations. He held the French Legion of Honour, the Red Eagle of Prussia, the Crown of Württemberg and the Leopold of Austria.

In addition to his estate at Vileiskoye, near Minsk, Wylie had received an additional 7,120 roubles a year for his long service. His many presents included a diamond ring and snuff box from Tsar Nicholas as well as a magnificent coach. In Russia he was regarded as one of the most prominent men of his day.

Most bizarrely, from Appleby's *Caledonian Phalanx*, comes the claim that Wylie was even honoured by Napoleon. This may, however, refer to the pair of pistols he is known to have possessed, taken some time either during or after the retreat from Moscow.

CHAPTER THIRTY-NINE

The Last Days

Wylie was living in his own house in Galerney when the American Doctor William Channing arrived in St Petersburg in the spring of 1854, just before the war with France and Britain began. He left a description of what he found within the house.

> The rooms about which I wandered were singularly deficient in furniture but on the walls were some pictures . . . At length the servant reappeared and asked me to follow him to Sir James. Upon entering the room my whole attention was attracted by the figure of a very tall old man between eighty and ninety stretched at full length upon a sofa.'
>
> 'Let me know how I can serve you,' said Sir James, without attempting to rise.

Channing then told him that he wished to visit the civil and military hospitals, whereupon Sir James replied that a doctor with the rank of colonel would call on him in the morning and take him to all the hospitals he wished to see.

It appears quite plain from the American's journal that he and the old Scotsman struck up an immediate rapport. Channing continues to recount how hardly a day passed during his visit to St Petersburg when he did not visit Sir James. Although obviously frail, his mind was clear and he talked much of his experiences during the war with Napoleon when he had seen so many battlefields, nearly always in company with Tsar Alexander, the man of whom in retrospect he spoke with the reverence due almost to a god. Particularly he told of Leipzig, when Alexander himself had so narrowly escaped fatal injury from the cannon ball which, hurtling through the body of Count Moreau's horse, had destroyed both of its rider's legs. He described how, with no alternative, he had amputated both of the limbs: the death of the count, although inevitable, still seemed to lie heavy on the physician's mind.

On a more cheerful note he told his servant to bring the patent of the baronetcy, which Channing understood had been conferred upon him on the battlefield, although actually it had been on Ascot Heath. Perhaps, by this time, bewildered by so many reminiscences, one or both of them was becoming slightly confused. He also showed the American all the decorations and orders he had received from the many monarchs he had served.

On another day something was said which took him back to his boyhood and his servant was sent to bring him 'a certain package which was very carefully opened and its contents showed to me. "Here," said Sir James, "are my school books. My first writing books, my ciphering books, and these are my mathematical manuscripts. You see I have kept them all." ' His visitor was amazed by the condition of these notebooks, in which the writing was so neat and precise and the paper still almost as good as new, although slightly yellowed with age.

Sadly, Wylie then described how his memoirs, compiled it would seem in his retirement, had been destroyed on the orders of the tsar. 'The emperor had directed it,' was all he said.

Why, one wonders, did he obey? Channing was probably the first to be horrified to hear that such an irreplaceable record of Russian history had been lost to the world. Rational explanations remain hard to find, but it can only be surmised that it was the fear of exposure of his grandfather's undoubted madness, or else a paranoid terror of publicity, which made Tsar Nicholas, whom Wylie had known from his childhood, condemn to the flames an autobiography of such enormous interest.

On the day before he left St Petersburg, Channing paid his last visit to Galerney Street where, to his great distress, he found Sir James Wylie very ill.

He had passed a wretched night and was breathing with so much agony, and was so exhausted, that he could hardly raise his hand to me or say farewell. He was stretched out on the sofa, as he was when I first saw him, and it seemed impossible that he would ever rise from it again. I thanked him for all the kindness he had showed me and took my leave. It was not without sadness, this leave-taking at the borders of the grave.

Wylie died on 2 March 1854. Although a public figure, his private life remains mysterious, hidden by the web of secrecy that he himself did much to preserve.

From the available evidence it would seem that his abiding passion was complete absorption in his work. It is said that he found recreation in gymnastics and bodily exercises, that his favourite sports were swimming, horse-riding, fencing, ice-skating, billiards and hunting. His intellectual interests, however, were limited due to the fact that his immense workload all but monopolized his time.

In mid-life he was described as being stout, with a confident appearance and robust health. His height of 1.88m and his thin red hair marked him as a northerner.[98] The same source continues that his character was distinguished by a number of valuable qualities: straightforwardness and candour, enormous diligence and persistence, confidence and skill in communicating with other people. In Russian literature he is known as an excellent organizer and administrator, with a quick and supple mind.[99]

Despite this, he had detractors. He is said to have been both arrogant and conceited, a sycophantic courtier 'who hung upon the lips of the most powerful and surrounded himself with flatterers . . . patronising friendliness alternated with fits of anger where he could be wrong and unjust and reveal all his contempt for those under him'.[100]

Is this the voice of truth, or rather the jibes of colleagues whose jealousy remained unquenched? Certainly it must be remembered that even Doctor Lyall, while deriding Wylie's capabilities as a doctor, nonetheless admitted that none did more for the Russian soldier than he.

Wylie's undying attachment to Alexander seems, in fact, to have been based on a near paternal relationship with a man so vulnerable to depression and illness as to be almost dependent on his support. Over and above this, despite his human weaknesses, and perhaps because of the courage with which he faced the demons besetting his mind, Wylie greatly admired the emperor to whom he became indispensable both as physician and friend.

Wylie was by then known to be eccentric, careful with his money and fiercely protective of his privacy. Suffice it to say that, at least when living in the Winter Palace, he was perfectly happy with the company of his dogs, existing, when not asked out to dine, on black bread and salt. Respected and to some extent feared in old age, he died with the secrets of his own life, and the knowledge of what really happened to Emperor Alexander whose trust, under no circumstances, would he ever betray.

He certainly had planned at one point to return to Scotland for at least part of the year. His great-niece testifies to his having been 'seized in a tenement of houses in Kincardine in April 1823 belonging to the sequestered estate of George Millar, shipmaster, to whom he had given two loans of £150 each'. Confirming his intentions he had asked Mr Edward, a Dundee merchant, husband of his niece, who came to visit him in Russia in June 1839, 'to look out for a suitable property'. He had, he assured him, 'no desire to leave Russia and return permanently to Scotland' but wished to have a home in his native land where he could enjoy 'a month or two of sport in an interesting district'. He thought of buying Harviestoun Estate, near Dollar, and actually began negotiations for purchasing Glenogil near Kirriemuir, the difficulty being that he did not want a large house, 'knowing from experience that such is the cause of considerable annoyance and anxiety', as he told his niece. Nevertheless, planning to buy land in Scotland he invested £50,000 in British bonds at 3 per cent in order to have money readily available.

Mrs Edwards, to whom he spoke with great affection of his relatives in Scotland, was obviously a favourite among them. Her uncle gave her a valuable diamond ring, which he himself had been given by Catherine the Great, while her husband departed with a Siberian topaz and a seal that had been presented to the doctor by Emperor Alexander. Later Mrs Edwards was to receive a very fine Persian cloak, a pocket Bible which his mother had given him, his portrait and one of the medals that had been struck on the orders of Tsar Nicholas on the occasion of celebrations in St Petersburg to mark the fiftieth anniversary of Wylie's service under the Russian government.

Two sons of his eldest brother William (the schoolmaster in Dundee) who went out to visit their uncle in Russia prospered greatly, while William's grandson (son of the minister of Carluke whom Wylie had tried to persuade to return with him to Russia) 'was for many years one of the most respected citizens of St Petersburg'. It would seem that it was William, father of Wylie's great-niece, who, 'when a sailor boy in St Petersburg', was given 'a large silver pen and pen holder which combined a mathematical instrument',[101] and David Wylie, a son of Sir James's brother Robert, died in Moscow in 1836.[102]

Sir James Wylie, who died aged eighty-six, was buried in the Volchoff burial ground in St Petersburg. While his nephew George was the chief mourner, his funeral was attended by the tsar and all the members of the court, regardless of the fact that war between Russia and Wylie's native country was just about to be declared. Having never married he left no direct descendants, but the money he had invested in British bonds, with the idea of buying an estate in Scotland, was eventually divided among his relations. A case raised in the Court of Chancery by Walter, his only surviving brother, decreed that under British law this money could not be alienated to a foreign power.

The residue of his fortune, valued at 1.5 million roubles, however, went to the Emperor Nicholas and the Russian nation specifically for the building of 'a large hospital at St Petersburg to be attended by the pupils of the Medico-Chirurgical Academy'.[103]

Five years after his death, when the Christmas Day of 1859 fell on the seventy-ninth anniversary of the enrolment of the young doctor from Scotland to the Eletsky Regiment, a monument in the courtyard of the Wylie Clinical Hospital was dedicated to his memory. It shows him sitting on a rock, in the parade uniform of an army surgeon, with his book on 'Military Pharmacy' at his feet. In his left hand he holds a paper scroll; in his right a pencil. The statue, cast in bronze, stands on a pedestal of black Finnish marble carved with emblems of Hygeia, the Greek goddess of health. One of the four sides shows Wylie's coat of arms, designed for him by Tsar Alexander himself. Another is a representation of the first meeting of the academy, a third depicts him saving wounded on the battlefield, and a fourth bears the dedicatory inscription.

The Mayakovskaya Hospital, built to Wylie's memory with the money he had left, was opened in 1873. Designed in the shape of a W in his honour, it contained 150 beds of which 120 were free and the remainder for paying patients. Today the hospital holds departments of haematology and clinical immunology, with the clinical oncology of non-Hodgkin's lymphoma increasingly significant.

And so in Russia the doctor from Scotland, so largely forgotten in his own country, is remembered not only as a medical pioneer and personal physician to three tsars, but as the man who, by introducing field hospitals, saved thousands of soldiers from dying untended on the battlefields, as Russia fought for survival against Napoleon's might.

Envoi

Less than a year had passed since the death of Sir James Wylie when, on 24 February 1855, the news of his army's disasters in Eupatoria reached Tsar Nicholas I. According to Doctor Mandt, the tsar's new personal physician, this 'stunned him and struck the fatal blow. "How many lives sacrificed in vain!" he murmured sadly while speaking of his poor soldiers.'

From that moment on, according to his doctor, the tsar refused to eat, and handed over almost all of his responsibilities, particularly those not concerned with the army, to his eldest son, the Grand Duke Alexander. Very shortly after this he developed a cold that turned into influenza. However, none of Doctor Mandt's warnings that it was dangerous would stop him from going out, wearing only an overcoat, to the huge and draughty riding school to review and say farewell to a detachment of Guards Infantry about to leave for Lithuania.

The result, as Mandt had predicted, was that his virus turned into pneumonia. He asked several of his generals to come and say goodbye to him and begged the tsarevich to say goodbye for him to the Guards, the army and, above all, to the heroic defenders of Sevastopol. 'Tell them that in the other world I will continue to pray for them. I have always striven to work for their good. If it has not always succeeded, it was not for lack of goodwill, but for want of knowledge and ability. I beg them to forgive me.'[104]

Nicholas I died on the morning of 4 March 1855. Inevitably rumours spread that he had poisoned himself with Mandt's assistance, but as in the case of his brother's death, there is no concrete evidence to support these claims. Nicholas was born in 1796, at much the same time as a young James Wylie had become his father's personal physician. He did at least reach his sixtieth year, a lifespan twelve years longer than that of the brother he had succeeded to the throne.

Nicholas's dying wish that his soldiers should be cared for was in part carried out by his sister-in-law, the Grand Duchess Elena, wife of his youngest brother Michael, who although unhappily married, or perhaps as a result of this, became as dedicated as Florence Nightingale, saviour of British soldiers, to nursing the sick and wounded Russians on the battlefield.

Therefore, it must be said that the human suffering and loss of life resulting from nineteenth-century European wars did at least bring enlightenment to medical practice regardless of the nationality of the doctors and nurses whose dedication saved the lives of these hitherto neglected men.

Notes

1. Müller-Dietz, H., *J. Wylie and the Medico-Chirurgical Academy in St Petersburg*, p. 15.
2. Meiklejohn, The Rev. William, *Tulliallan: Four Lads o' Pairts*, p. 1.
3. Sheriff Court Records of Clackmannan.
4. Müller-Dietz. H., p. 1
5. Meiklejohn, Rev. W., p. 15, note 7.
6. Ibid., p. 2.
7. 1996 *Scottish Medical Journal*. Paper by A.A. Novik, V.I. Mazurov & P. d'A Semple. 'The Life & Times of Sir James Wylie Bt., MD., 1768–1854'.
8. Doctor Clarke's Travels in Russia, Tartary and Turkey.
9. Troyat, Henri. *Catherine the Great*, pp. 319–20.
10. Troyat, Henri, p. 311.
11. A lithotomy is a surgical procedure for removing stones from organs such as the bladder or kidney.
12. Müller-Dietz. H., p. 2.
13. Ibid.
14. Masson. F., *Memoirs of Catherine II and the Court*, pp. 145–8.
15. Palmer, A., *Life of Alexander I*, p. 30.
16. Almedingen, E.M., *The Emperor Alexander I*, p. 60.
17. Appleby, John H., *Through the Looking-Glass: Scottish Doctors in Russia (1704–1854)*, pp. 60-61.
18. Troyat, H., *Catherine the Great*, pp. 322–3.
19. Appleby, J.H., p. 61.
20. Meiklejohn, Rev. W., p. 15.
21. Tooke, *Life of Catherine II*, Vol.1.
22. Palmer, A., p. 45.
23. Joyneville, C., *Life and Times of Alexander I*, Vol. III, p. 364.
24. Palmer, A., p. 65.
25. Palmer, A., p. 102.
26. Palmer, A., p. 109.
27. Guthrie, Matthew, *Supplementary Tour*, p. 48.

28. Palmer. A., p. 138.

29. Almedingen, E.M., *The Emperor Alexander*, p. 101.

30. Müller-Dietz, H., p. 3.

31. Adam, A., *FRCS. Aberdeen Royal Infirmary*, ed I. Levack and H. Dudley, 1992.

32. Thomson, Anthony Todd. *Elements of Materia Medica and Therapeutics*.

33. A verst = 3,500 yards, or about three quarters of a mile.

34. Palmer, A., p. 203.

35. Lieven, D., *Russia against Napoleon*, p. 157.

36. Ibid., p. 186.

37. Tolstoy, L., *War and Peace, Part 2*, p. 902.

38. Palmer, A., p. 248.

39. Palmer, A., p. 253.

40. Lieven, D., p. 286.

41. Palmer, A., p. 260.

42. Meiklejohn, the Rev. W., p. 6.

43. Müller-Dietz, H., p. 3.

44. Lieven, D., p. 416.

45. Fremont-Barnes, Gregory., *The Napoleonic Wars*, (4), p. 48.

46. Palmer, A., p. 273.

47. Lieven, D., p. 143.

48. Joyneville. C., Vol III. p. 26.

49. Meiklejohn, Rev. W., p. 9.

50. Meiklejohn, Rev. W., p. 16.

51. Palmer, A., pp. 296–7.

52. Ibid., p. 298.

53. Müller-Dietz, H., p. 7.

54. Novik, Mazurov, Semple, p. 119

55. Schuster, Norah H., *Paper Records of British Medical Society*, Vol. 61, February 1968, p. 185.

56. Palmer, A., p. 319.

57. Palmer, A., p. 324.

58. Joyneville, C., p. 196.

59. Palmer, A., p. 332.

60. £1 = approximately 473 roubles.

61. Novik, Mazurov, Semple, p. 118.

62. One rouble is divided into 100 copecks (kopeks).

63. Meiklejohn, Rev. W., p. 7.

64. Lyall, Robert, *Travels in Russia, the Crimea, the Caucusus, and Georgia*, Vol. II. pp. 425–6.

65. Meiklejohn, Rev. W., p. 5.
66. Ibid., p. 114.
67. Novik, Mazurov, Semple, p. 117.
68. Palmer, A., p. 344.
69. Almedingen, E.M., p. 175.
70. Almedingen, E.M., p. 181.
71. Joyneville, C., p. 275.
72. Pope-Hennessey, Una, *Alexandra Memoir*, pp. 44–5.
73. Palmer, A., p. 166
74. Joyneville, C., p. 318.
75. Lee, Doctor R., 'The Last Days of Alexander I and the First Days of Nicholas I' Item 206.
76. Palmer, A., p. 382.
77. Palmer, A., p. 77.
78. Joyneville, C., p. 347 (footnote).
79. Troubetzkoy, A.S., *Imperial Legend*, p. 126.
80. *Russkaya Starina* magazine, Vol. 73 (1892), p. 79.
81. Magazine editor suggests Severski.
82. Lee, R., p. 15.
83. This is the second time that Alexander's fondness for Scottish reels, presumably taught to him by Wylie, is mentioned.
84. Ibid., p. 27.
85. The castle built at Alupka, in both English and Gothic style, now an art gallery and museum, and where Winston Churchill stayed during the Yalta Conference, was at that time only being planned.
86. Over four miles.
87. From *Russkaya Starina*, Vol. 3 (1892), p. 79.
88. Alexander I was born on 12 December 1777 (Julian calendar).
89. Appleby, J., *The Caledonian Phalanx, Scots in Russia*, p. 63.
90. Lee, R., p. 66.
91. Troubetzkoy, A.S., p. 191.
92. Troubetzkoy, A.S., p. 192.
93. Troubetzkoy, A.S., pp. 246–7.
94. Ibid.
95. Lee, R., p. 125.
96. One wonders if she made them stop to see it!
97. Meiklejohn, Rev. W., p. 12.
98. Müller-Dietz, H., p. 6.
99. Ibid.
100. Ibid., p. 7.

101. Meiklejohn, Rev. W., p. 12.
102. Ibid.
103. Novik, Mazurov, Semple, p. 119.
104. de Grunwald, C., *Tsar Nicholas II*, p. 284.

Bibliography

Almedingen, E.M. *The Emperor Alexander 1*, The Bodley Head, London 1964

Appleby, J.H. *Through The Looking Glass: Scottish Doctors in Russia (1704–1854) The Caledonian Phalanx*, British Library Document Supply Centre, Official Publications 18 Dec. 1987 GPB-8867

George, Hereford B, *Napoleon's Invasion of Russia*, T Fisher Unwin, 1899

de Grunwald, Constantin, *Tsar Nicholas I: The Life of an Absolute Monarch*, The Alcuin Press, Welwyn Garden City, 1954

Hutchison, Sir R., MD., FRCP, A Medical Adventurer (biographical note on Sir James Wylie, Bt., MD 1758 to 1854)

Joynville, *Life and Times of Alexander I*, vols. 1–3, Elibron Classics (unabridged facsimile of the edition, Tinsley Brothers, London 1875)

Lancet, March 18 1854

Lee, Robert, FRCS, *The Last Days of Alexander and the First Days of Nicholas (Emperors of Russia)* Richard Bentley, London 1854

Lieven, D., *The Battle for Europe 1807 to 1814*, Penguin 2009

Lincoln, W. Bruce., *Nicholas I Emperor and Autocrat of All the Russias*, Northern Illinois University Press, 1989

Lyall, R. *Travels in Russia*, vol. ii. 1825, *British and Foreign Medical Review*, 1836

Meiklejohn, Rev. William, *Four Lads o'Pairts*, pub. privately 1990

Moss., Walter G., *A History of Russia*, vol. 1: To 1917, McGraw-Hill Primis Custom Publishing 2001

Mülller-Dietz, H. J., *J. Wylie und die medico-chirurgische Akademie in St Petersburg*, in *Clio Medica* 4, 1969

Novik, A.A. Mazurov, V.I., d'A., Semple, P., *The Life and Times of Sir James Wylie Bt., MD. 1768–1854, Body Surgeon and Physician to the Tsar* and *Chief of the Russian Military Medical Department*, pub privately (extract from *Scottish Medical Journal* 1996; 41: pp. 116–120)

Oxford Dictionary of National Biography, OUP 2004

Palmer, A., *Alexander I, Tsar of War and Peace*, Weidenfield and Nicholson, London 1974

Robertson, Edna, *Glasgow' Doctor*, Tuckwell Press, East Linton 1998

Russell, William Howard, *The British Expedition to the Crimea*, Elibron Classics Adamant Media Corporation 2005

Troubetzkoy, Alexis S, *Imperial Legend, The Mysterious Disappearance of Tsar Alexander I*, Arcade Publishing, New York 2002

Troyat, Henri, *Caherine The Great*, translated Joan Pinkham, First Meridian Printing 1994

Index

Index